Letters
to
Uncle Mike

by
Michael Burgess

Saddle Mountain Press

ISBN 0-9657638-5-4

Second Printing

Printed in the United States of America

Published by:
Saddle Mountain Press
P. O. Box 1096
Cannon Beach, OR 97110
Phone (503) 436-2947
Fax (503) 436-8635

Email: saddlemountain@upperleftedge.com

Cover designed by Anderson McConaughy, Portland, Oregon.

The paper used in this publication meets the minimum requirements of
American National Standard. ANSI Z 39.48-1984

Acknowledgments

The author owes much to many people. Stop squirming in your seat. Neither he nor Uncle Mike confuse the publication of a second edition to 'Letters to Uncle Mike' with the Academy Award ceremonies. Life is too brief and we're all too busy for anything but a short list.

First, to Billy Hults, editor of the Upper Left Edge, the New Yorker of the northern Oregon Coast. It was Billy who first published Ask Uncle Mike and it was his wildly not for profit arts foundation, the Left Coast Group, that, hoping to make a buck peddling free advice, published the first edition. You may be sure he spent some of the nonprofits on beer. He certainly didn't spend them on me. Unless you count the all expense paid trip to baseball spring training in Tempe. And, had you been there, you might not count it either.

Next, to Bob and Susann Ragsdale who, contrary to good business sense and the advice of many who love them, are the new owners and publishers of Saddle Mountain Press. They are, small surprise, very odd and wonderful people. At times, alarmingly so. Our business meetings at Bill's Tavern in Cannon Beach never fail to inspire me to spend even more time being in good company. Bob, it should be mentioned, is also my mentor in the application of quantum mechanics to the art of stud poker. Yes, if you must know, we attend a weekly poker support group that includes Billy Hults. This does not necessarily make us cronies.

And finally, my sincere thanks to the many people who wrote, and continue to write, to Uncle Mike. Uncle Mike often worries about you but he's grateful nonetheless.

Dedication

This book is dedicated to my father and mother,
Jay and Wanda, and to Jason, my son.
And to Easy, my old black lab, who taught me much.

Introduction

For several years now, Uncle Mike has written a freeform advice column from his offices at the Upper Left Edge---a post-journalism monthly that focuses on small affairs and slow breaking events from its vantage point in Cannon Beach, a small village on the Oregon Coast. How he came to dispense personal advice with no more credentials than a worried love for the human comedy is a story worth telling. Or would be, if Uncle Mike thought it concerned you.

Letters To Uncle Mike

Dear Uncle Mike,

I'm a 32 year old professional woman, married, with no children. Both my husband and I own our own businesses. Last year, mine did quite well and, to celebrate, I want to trade in my Camry on a Miata. Brad says if I get a new car, he gets one too. His mother, the old harpy, calls at least twice a week to say I'm being selfish and unfair. I say it's my money and I can spend it however I want. If Brad wants a new car, let him earn it. There's not a thing wrong with his BMW. I say he's being childish, what do you think?

Celeste

Dear Celeste,

Uncle Mike thinks you and Brad should get a used VW bus and set off in search of a life.

● ● ●

Dear Uncle Mike,

My old girlfriend told me I was sexist macho slime. So, I went to counseling, squared myself away and became a sensitive, supportive male. My new girlfriend says I'm a wuss. Is there some part of this I'm not getting?

Celibate

Dear Celibate,

Several parts, probably. First, stop listening to women for whom your sociosexual identity is an agenda item. Trust me, there's a better than even chance you know as much about being a man as they do. Uncle Mike also recommends you find a new companion. The one you're seeing obviously needs a little time alone. Uncle Mike recommends you open the door for her.

● ● ●

Dear Uncle Mike,

I recently won the lottery. Not the big one, but enough so I don't have to work for a few years if I don't want to. And I don't. Here's the problem, I'm a 28 year old woman, single, and reasonably attractive. Suddenly, my boyfriend thinks we should move in together. He's even talking about marriage. Guys are coming out of the woodwork. It's getting so stupid, I've thought of leaving town. Who can you trust?

Wary

Dear Wary,

Listen very carefully to Uncle Mike. You can't trust anyone. Your boyfriend sounds as sincere as a hungry alligator. As for the men swarming outside your window, they are, at best, the piranha of mandom. They'll spend your money, use you badly, then toss you aside like a corn cob. Leaving town is a splendid idea. There are men out there who'll love you just because you're you. Uncle Mike thinks we should meet for cocktails.

Dear Uncle Mike,

My husband John has been stealing my underwear. I don't have a lot, so I notice when a pair of panties is missing for a day or two then suddenly reappears in the laundry. He denies everything. At first I thought I was going nuts but, since we don't have children, nobody else could be doing it. The idea of John wearing my underwear neither repulses me nor turns me on. He's a wonderful man and all I want is a little honesty. Any suggestions?

Crossed Dresser

Dear Cross,

First, let Uncle Mike assure you there's nothing at all wrong with John wearing your knickers. Weird, certainly, but not wrong. Party frocks on the street would be another matter. Your real problem is that your husband is a sneak thief. This is not a trait that will go away by itself. Uncle Mike suggests you give John boy one more chance to come out of your drawers. If he demurs, come to bed in his boxer shorts. Let Uncle Mike know how it turns out.

● ● ●

Dear Uncle Mike,

My lady friend and I are having problems. Maybe you can help. We're both in our mid-twenties and have been seeing (sleeping with) each other for a few months. She's beautiful and I love her and all, but I'm just not ready for a long-term commitment. I've still got some

3

wild oats to sow and she's starting to lay the monogamy guilt trip on me. I say men aren't built either physically or hormonally to be monogamous. What do you think?

Born Free

Dear Born Stupid,

Uncle Mike is suddenly very tired. He wonders if you might have heard of AIDS, the sexually transmitted plague that still promises to make the Dark Ages seem like a romp? Given that women contract HIV virus from men more readily than men contract it from women, your partner would have to have the brains of a crowbar not to ask for, and expect, fidelity. What do you imagine? She wants to die a lingering death?

As for male humans being genetically incapable of keeping their pants on: horsepucky. You're confusing yourself with a gerbil, perhaps for good reason. Contrary to the impression you make in your letter, Uncle Mike must assume you're capable of simple reason. If you wouldn't bet your partner's life on a hand of three card monte, you must choose not to behave like a weasel in rut.

Whether you stay in this relationship or not (and Uncle Mike hopes with all his heart the young lady drops you like a hot stone), the rest of us on the planet would love you to buy a volume of good Victorian erotica, or maybe a Sports Illustrated swimsuit issue, and sow your wild oats by hand.

●●●

Dear Uncle Mike,

As a nonsmoker, I resent very much that your picture shows you holding a cigarette. Smoking has been proven to be both a personal and public health hazard. Your endorsement of this disgusting and dangerous habit is not just an insult, it is a deadly assault upon those of us who must suffer and die from your addiction.

Fed Up

Dear Fed Up,

We all suffer darling, believe me. Yes, Uncle Mike smokes. He also drinks sour mash whiskey and plays poker. They are part of his religion. Your whining is two-pronged. As regards the personal dangers of inhaling tobacco smoke, when Uncle Mike last looked, George Burns was still breathing at ninety. Cancer is a disease of the immune system. The immune system is savaged by stress. To Uncle Mike's way of thinking, this makes worrying about smoking as deadly as doing it.

As for endangering innocent victims, think for a moment dear. Do you truly believe in your self-righteous little heart that my smoking a cigarette, even at the next table, ranks with exhaust pipes? Please. Like several people he knows, and most other people on the planet, Uncle Mike doesn't own a car. He regards driving as a filthy and disgusting habit. Did you know the average car belches out its curb weight in carbon monoxide every year, sweets? If you need to march somewhere with your pitchfork, Uncle Mike suggests your garage.

●●●

5

Letters to Uncle Mike

Dear Uncle Mike,

I feel silly asking for advice, but I'm having a real problem with my husband's mother. We've had a good relationship until now but, since my son Dylan turned five, things have gone to hell. For his birthday, Dylan got a kiddie harness from a girlfriend of mine. He looks cute as a bug in it, and it's a great help when I go shopping. Alice, my mother-in-law, has all but stopped speaking to me. She says only dogs have leashes. I say she's out of touch. What do you think?

Tina in Newport

Dear Tina,

Uncle Mike thinks you need professional help. If, at the age of five, your son Dylan needs to leashed, either he or you need to be put to sleep.

Uncle Mike finds it both curious and chilling that your husband (old What's His Name) doesn't figure somewhere in the discussion. So you and Alice are duking it out to see if your apprentice adult male's first memories involve being led around on a leash by the woman he most trusts. How very charming. If you're worried young Dylan might stray at the mall, Uncle Mike suggests you train him to voice commands. Or, if this fails, a whistle.

●●●

Dear Uncle Mike,

In your last column, you made a big deal about not owning a car. What does this make you? Holy? Give me a break. You ecocreeps make me puke.

Marvin in Taft

6

Dear Marv,

Sorry you're feeling poorly. Instead of going for your idiot throat, a path Uncle Mike is sorely tempted to take, he'll tell you instead a story attributed to the Nobel physicist Werner Heisenberg.

A traveler in a backward country comes across an aged peasant hoeing his field. Amused, the traveler asks the bumpkin if he's never heard of machines.

"I have heard my teacher say," the old man answered, "that whoever uses machines does all his work like a machine. He who does his work like a machine grows a heart like a machine, and he who carries the heart of a machine in his breast loses his simplicity. He who loses his simplicity becomes unsure in the strivings of his soul. Uncertainty in the strivings of the soul is something which does not agree with honest sense. It is not that I do not know of such things. I am ashamed to use them."

As regards holiness, Uncle Mike prefers hollowness. He also loves to walk.

●●●

Dear Uncle Mike,

My girlfriend and I just moved in together and want to get a pet. Cats and dogs are a little common and we're anything but. We think it would be way cool to get something different. We've decided on some kind of exotic poisonous snake. Can you train snakes not to bite?

Kyle and Chrissy, Beaverton

Dear Nitwits,

Listen very carefully to Uncle Mike. You're poised on the brink of the biggest, and perhaps last, mistake of your bored little lives. In the first place, no one normal lives with a snake. Normal people avoid snakes. The two of you should chant this several times a day.

Should you choose to go through with this madness, don't plan to entertain. Or, if your snake is a large constrictor, or a pit viper of any size, to sleep. By the same law of nature that ensures anything dropped in the bathroom will land in the toilet, your snake will eventually escape from its terrarium. And that, as they say, will be that. Herpophiles, who tend to smile and weave when they talk, will tell you snakes are smart as whips and, contrary to common belief, friendly to a fault. For the balanced and thoughtful, these are not selling points. Uncle Mike strongly recommends you not snuggle with your pet. Regardless how friendly your rattlesnake seems, its interests won't always coincide with yours. Sooner rather than later, push will come to shove, and things will turn ugly fast. The best advice Uncle Mike can give you is to overfeed your snake, move slowly, and never put down your machete.

● ● ●

Dear Uncle Mike,

If you could be any kind of tree you wanted, which one would you be?

A Fan in Tillamook

Dear Bored Person,

One whose pulp is not turned into People Magazine or Newt Gingrich's next book. Did you read, by the way, that Little Fib Newton didn't actually write To Renew America? And that the guy who did spent a whole two weeks crafting it?

● ● ●

Dear Uncle Mike,

My vacation's coming up and I can't decide where to go that I haven't already been. Any favorite hideaways you'd like to recommend?

Restless in Salem

Dear Restless,

Uncle Mike regrets he can be no help shaping your itinerary. Being fiscally challenged, Uncle Mike tends to winter where he summers. The last madcap getaway he took was to Phoenix with Reverend Billy for spring training, a term having meaning only to baseball persons. Reverend Billy, poor baby, is a Cubs fan. Uncle Mike, who often confuses baseball and golf, spent six days drinking Bombay tonics by the pool. It charged his batteries nicely.

● ● ●

Dear Uncle Mike,

My six year old daughter Brie is an absolute gem, but lately she's become a fussy eater. After years of giving her whatever she wants to eat, within reason of course, she now refuses to eat anything she hasn't seen on television. She's very determined, especially about broccoli which they've found is quite good for us. What should I do?

Perplexed in Netarts

Dear Perplexed,

Uncle Mike assumes you've ruled out having your daughter adopted by an intelligent adult.

Give Uncle a freaking break. The 'very determined' human you're dealing with is six years old. You are, if not smarter than she, at least larger and, in the normal scheme of things, in charge. Point this out often to the little tyrant. You should also turn off the television set and stop obsessing about broccoli. When children get hungry, they eat. Even if there's nothing around but good food.

● ● ●

Dear Uncle Mike,

I think my husband is cheating on me. Late nights at the office, Saturdays he says he needs for himself, a dreamy look sometimes when he's shaving. We've been together for ten years and I know we love each other. It would be hard, but I could live with knowing he's having an affair. What I can't live with is dishonesty. What should I do?

End of My Rope in Toledo

Dear Rope,

Uncle Mike has heard many stories of wives and husbands who wanted the truth. In his experience, what they really wanted was for the truth to stop. Try this. Schedule a scented bath together. Candlelight and a flirtatious Beaujolais. Tickle your mate's tummy with your toe and ask, one last time, if he's been jumping the fence. When he says no, and Uncle Mike would be willing to bet his mother's pension that he will, tell him you think he's lying through his teeth. Grab a soft body part and explain you're considering either gelding him in his sleep or taking up with a young buck. And that he's got a week to talk you out of it.

● ● ●

Dear Uncle Mike,

On our way to dinner the other night, my friend and I were approached by a panhandler. My friend gave him a quarter. I say she's a chump who just became a codependent and the guy probably just spent it on booze or dope. What do you think?

Shirley in Portland

Dear Shirley,

About what? Do I think the human you feel so superior to raced off with your friend's quarter for a night of debauchery? What should he do? Save it for a down payment on an Infiniti?

Mostly, Uncle Mike thinks it's not his business, or

yours. He suggests you review the definitions of "charity" and "gift." If Uncle Mike found himself standing on the corner asking strangers for money, he might need a drink too. If you can't spare a quarter to make someone's load a little lighter, at least spare us your Calvinist moralizing. Uncle Mike sincerely hopes your job is secure.

●●●

Dear Uncle Mike,
Our daughter Jennifer is five. Several months ago, my wife read her a book about fairies. Ever since, Jennifer insists she sees and hears them all around her. Her mother is beside herself and wants Jennifer to see a therapist. I say she'll outgrow it. Do other kids go through this?
Art in Netarts

Dear Art,
Not nearly enough. There's nothing wrong with little Jennifer, she just sees things you don't. Cats interact with "nothing" all the time and we think its charming. When kids do it, we give them Prozac. For what it's worth, people have believed in faeries for thousands of years. Uncle Mike can't bring himself to think they were all lunatics. The faerie faith, that branch of animism that flowered in Europe, rests on the belief that nature, all of it, is alive. Physicists now regard this as a fair assessment of the truth. Are there faeries? If your

daughter sees them there are. Before you shuffle the poor kid off to the dream killers, think on this. If no one's ever seen an electron, and they haven't, how much more real are they than elves?

● ● ●

Dear Uncle Mike,
    If, as Nils Bohr said, atoms aren't "things," and the universe is made of atoms, then it can't be a "thing" either, right? If all there is "no thing," how come there's anything?

Marv in Newport

Dear Marv,
    Tricky question, babe. If you ask me, Von Neumann was right. The unmanifest potential of deep reality is collapsed into the observable object/events of the quantum world by consciousness, defined as the awareness of difference. Since Von Neumann's Proof (1932), it hasn't been possible to frame the rules of observed reality without reference to consciousness, the perceptual ghost in the machine. As Heisenberg said, "There is no quantum reality. There is only an abstract description of it." Without the awareness of difference, the necessary construct lying behind the world and all its equations, the universe becomes Gertrude Stein's Oakland. There's no there, there.

● ● ●

Dear Uncle Mike,

My girlfriend and I have been debating our positions for a month now and have agreed to let you decide. Is it politically correct for a man to open a door for a woman? She says it's a male power trip, I say it's just being polite. What do you think?

Brad and Sherrie in Eugene

Dear Buffy and Muffy,

Having never quite grasped political correctness, Uncle Mike opens doors for women all the time. He also lights their cigarettes, buys them lunch, and compliments their appearance. Most have the good grace to say thank you.

Uncle Mike quarrels with the notion that relations between men and women must always boil down to a power struggle. Certainly we seem fated to commit mutual emotional atrocities stemming from hormone toxicity and fear of being alone, but this scarcely means we can't be friends, or that we shouldn't, in these times of war, practice reciprocal niceties. Opening doors is one of them.

Uncle Mike would never suggest that Norman Mailer's take on gender real politik is healthy or balanced, but he did say one cogent thing on the trench warfare between the sexes. "Most of the problems between the sexes would disappear if, every day, men told women they were beautiful and women told men they were brave."

For best results, the lines should be traded often.

● ● ●

Dear Uncle Mike,

A friend of mine who's been married for several years has started an affair with a woman at his office. I know his wife and like her a lot and I hate to see this happen. Should I butt in or butt out?

Leon in Seaside

Dear Leon,

Butt in. Uncle Mike is old enough to appreciate the healing power of a fling with someone who knows him just well enough to be excited. He also knows it ends in pain and sadness if a third person is involved. It often ends in pain and sadness anyway. Suggest to your friend that he stop toying with this new woman's affections and lying through his teeth to someone who's supposed to be his best friend. Being a hound may seem no end of fun, but it doesn't hold a candle to keeping your word to someone who trusts you.

● ● ●

Dear Uncle Mike,

My nephew is four. My sister and her husband call him spirited, I think he's a spoiled menace. Markie's latest cuteness is biting. We're talking ankles, fingers, and on one occasion, my buttocks. His mother laughs and tells Mark he's not being polite. Any suggestions?

Rabid in Newport

Dear Rabid,

Uncle Mike firmly believes in not contradicting the teachings of parents who are within earshot. Rather than creating a conflict in little Mark's budding conceptual framework, Uncle Mike suggests you wait for a quiet moment when the two of you are alone. Sit the little whelp on your knee, look him straight in the eye, and bite his thumb until he begs you to stop. Smile and tell him this is the lesson called "little dog and big dog." Ask if there's any part he doesn't understand.

● ● ●

Dear Uncle Mike,

Uncle Mike, my left buttock. What gives you the right to pass out advice? Are you an accredited counselor? I give better advice than you do and nobody pays me for it. Why don't you get a real job?

Earl in Albany

Dear Earl,

Thanks for taking the time to scrawl. Not to worry, the world hasn't deteriorated to the point that someone like Uncle Mike would be endorsed by any association of professional advice givers. Uncle Mike got the gig because he knows the publisher, Reverend Billy. And, more importantly, because he has photographs of a weekend in San Francisco Reverend Billy would like to forget.

Uncle Mike isn't the least bit surprised you give better advice than he does and is saddened you're not paid for it. Not saddened enough to give you his gig, but saddened nonetheless. As to why Uncle Mike doesn't go out and get a real job, he regards the term as an oxymoron. Uncle Mike has enough on his plate just figuring out what it means to be human.

••

Dear Uncle Mike,
    I went to my 30th high school reunion this summer and was shocked to see several of my male classmates with women my daughter's age on their arms. Aside from the obvious — boys will be boys and men will be old fools — what can they possibly see in these children? And don't these girls have fathers?
                                    Disgusted in Portland

Dear Disgusted,
    In a snit are we? Old fool that he is, Uncle Mike believes devoutly that love, like disgust, is where you find it. He also believes it's hard enough these days, when mating has become a shotgun marriage of Days of Our Lives and Let's Make A Deal, to find a friend and lover at all. Outlawing certain combinations is an unnecessary blow. One that, if enforced, would be fascist.
    What can men your age see in young women? Maybe someone not too jaded to be in love? Someone who finds them interesting? Someone who reminds him of the power of hopes and dreams? Someone who's not judging him through thirty years of sociosexual scar tissue?
    Uncle Mike winces at your reference to women in

17

their mid-twenties as children and weeps for your daughter. Humans, like cars, are best judged in terms of mileage. As for what your daughter might see in an older man, Uncle Mike would guess quite a bit.

Someone with manners, perhaps? Someone who knows how to order dinner in a place where one does it at a table? Someone able to carry on a conversation? Who's seen enough of life to value compassion and respect? Someone who'll listen to their dreams and fears without saying, "Sure, Babe"? Someone who's not a stranger to PMS? Someone wise enough to mind their own business?

● ● ●

Dear Uncle Mike,

Where do you stand on ET? Is there intelligent life in the universe? Are they friendly? Do they want to ravish our women and eat us?

Bill in Lincoln City

Dear Bill,

If, by ET, you mean lipless, doe-eyed, smooth skinned, salamander humanoids from Betelgeuse, Uncle Mike can only say he's never seen one. But then, Uncle Mike has never seen a Tasmanian. He saw someone from Los Angeles once. That was pretty interesting.

You ask if space aliens would be friendly. Uncle Mike would bet it depends. Everyone has off days and there are bad apples in every bushel. It would be alienist to generalize but Uncle Mike has a dispirited hunch their feelings for us would be much like ours for hamsters. It would be foolish to forget that any visitor from another planet would also most likely be a rich tourist or the representative of some government agency. This is not a win-win situation.

Would they ravish our womenfolk and turn us into sushi? Lord only knows. There are, after all, people in Newark who've done as much and not lost a minute's sleep. But Uncle Mike, ever the optimist, thinks it's more likely they'd take snapshots and ask penetrating questions about Rush Limbaugh.

Is there intelligent life in the universe? Do bears make poo in the woods? Uncle Mike believes the universe is an intelligent lifeform. There are, however, stupid reactions to it: a truth that nearly accounts for Kato Kaelin's new career.

●●●

Dear Uncle Mike,

I'm a single man, thirty something, and I think I'm a serial monogamist. I'm not a jerk or a user and people tell me I'm a nice guy. I totally enjoy my relationships with women, but they wind up being just episodes with a beginning, a middle, and an end. We both start off thinking this one's it, but something always fizzles for one or both of us. Is life a treadmill? Is there something here I'm not getting?

John in Nestucca

Letters to Uncle Mike

Dear John,

You've given Uncle Mike a tough nut to crack since, in your headlong rush to burden others with your problems, you neglected to say how serial your monogamy is. Since you assure Uncle Mike you're neither a jerk nor a predator, we'll assume your average relationship lasts longer than a night at the Red Lion. If so, you've experienced a series of brief marriages punctuated by brief divorces. In a world of unique stories, this isn't one of them. Having set your mind at ease, we press boldly on with your concerns.

First off, John boy, you're either a blithering idiot or a liar. You "totally" enjoy your relationships with women? Uncle Mike wonders if you do this while walking on water and healing the lame. Uncle Mike has no idea where you were during these relationships, but the truth of the matter is that male humans and female humans have a long history of not getting along. They may not have evolved on different planets but their madcap adventures in misunderstanding and vengeance have provided plots for Sophocles, Shakespeare, Woody Allen and, to a much lesser extent, Erica Jong.

Historically, men and women have stayed together, through thin and thin, in order to survive until the kids leave home. Neither gender thinks this is funny, or even necessary, anymore. Stupid, but there it is. Talk of love aside, the brave new freedoms that selfishness and irresponsibility bring account for the spontaneous decay of human pair bonds that is, along with the talk show, America's gift to the 21st century.

It's not the fact that your relationships have a beginning, a middle, and an end that should concern you. What process of nature doesn't progress through a cycle? It's your whining about it that bores Uncle Mike to tears. Although he's never pulled it off, Uncle Mike suspects the secret to mating for life is hiding in plain sight. You treat each other like friends and work for a common goal until one of you croaks.

● ● ●

Dear Uncle Mike,

I'm 26, I've got a great boyfriend, we get along fine and love each other. So what, you ask, is my problem? The rat bastard keeps looking at other women. He knows it makes me nuts. It's not like he's gross about it, but it's the thought that counts. Are all men hounds? You're a man. Go ahead and spout off.

Connie in Newberg

Dear Connie,

There seems to be a misunderstanding. Uncle Mike did not ask about your problems, you mailed them to him. Big difference, muffin. Are all men hounds? Absolutely not. Most of us only dream of it, a truth that makes us the Walter Mittys of dogdom. It can be a little sad sometimes.

With no intention of hurting your feelings, Uncle Mike would suggest you wake up and smell the mating instinct. The pomp and fury of gender correctness aside, we're still part of the wild kingdom. Without going into lurid anecdotes from his past, Uncle Mike recommends you pick up a good book on primate behavior and remember how cute your boyfriend looked howling outside your window.

Uncle Mike's no rocket psychologist but he's willing to bet that there's not a man on the planet who doesn't at least mentally gambol on strange lawns in the moonlight. Like the Mt. Everest of hormones, the lawns are just there. So is the call of the wild, which is to say, the different. The trick, as any domesticated male will admit when he's not moping, is to not act out one's ribald little fantasies on an unsuspecting world.

So the fact that your boyfriend looks at women only means he's neither blind nor dead. If you're looking for corrective measures (see: 'training'), Uncle Mike would suggest you not let your dog roam free at night, say "Good Boy" a lot, and give him treats when he doesn't ogle.

●●●

Dear Uncle Mike,

My girlfriend's thinking about getting breast implants. She's 25 and old enough to make her own decisions. It's okay by me if she wants bigger boobs, but are these things really safe?

Concerned in Bend

Dear Concerned,

Interesting word, boobs. Where have the years since high school gone? As Uncle Mike understands it, here's your question: Should the woman you love hire someone to slice open her breasts and shove in a pair of DEA approved whoopee cushions in order that she more closely resembles someone in a beer ad and, in so doing, enhance her sense of self worth?

Gee, that's a tough one. Being as kind as possible, and in this case it's a real strain, Uncle Mike doubts you or your friend have given matters sufficient thought. Actually, Uncle Mike wonders if either of you have the brains God gave a horseshoe.

If you love this woman, tell her to stay away from cosmeticians with knives. Sexual marketing ploys that involve self-mutilation are not the act of a rational person. Suggest she take the money her surgeon would (after making a mockery of her human dignity) spend on his Mercedes, and blow it instead on a week for the two of you someplace with palm trees, banana daiquiris, and massage oil. Someplace where you do nothing but invent new ways to tell her that the beauty granted to her by the elves of the universe is the only antidote to a poison you've taken. Under no circumstance, tell her it doesn't matter anyway because you're a thigh man.

● ● ●

Dear Uncle Mike,

My sister died recently and I'm taking it a little harder than I thought I would. She was okay with it mostly but there were times she was afraid and didn't want to leave. Now I'm wondering if all my lofty thoughts about next lives are just so much whistling past the graveyard. Any words of wisdom about death?

Alice R., Portland

Dear Alice,

Sorry, not a one. Having seen no evidence of death in nature, Uncle Mike doesn't believe in it, certainly not as defined by those with a personal stake in the promotion of mortal fear. Uncle Mike believes in change, not that he doesn't sometimes fight it tooth and claw, and in the question: from what to what?

Here's the thing, Alice. If you believe Einstein, the universe is a four-dimensional sphere in which the continuum of space/time is both closed and unbounded: an inside with no outside. Given this, Uncle Mike can't imagine where the dead would go. Ashes to ashes, dust to dust, the conservation of mass/energy and all that.

As for the spirit, Uncle Mike falls back on the rules of quantum cosmology set out so plainly in the Tibetan Book of the Dead and countless Zen koans. Freed from inertia (see: the Veil of Tears), the spirit (or point-conscious observer) expands. Slowly at first and then faster until it reaches the velocity of light.

As experiences go, this one's a doozy and Uncle Mike wouldn't miss it for the world. At velocity c, space/time (and with it the universe of perception) disappears in that endless nanosecond of bliss in which your mass becomes infinite and your perspective coterminal with all that is. And was, and ever shall be. It's not stretching matters to consider this event personally cosmic.

For what it's worth, Uncle Mike thinks Kahlil Gibran said all that needs to be said: "For what is it to die but to stand naked in the wind and to melt into the sun?" It may have been this that prompted Wendell Berry to write: "It is no tragedy when, at the end of a life, a man dies."

● ● ●

Dear Uncle Mike,

You made a nasty crack a while back about guys in Dockers beating drums and looking for the warrior within. What exactly is wrong, O guru my guru, with men getting in touch with the spirit of their masculinity?

Al in Astoria

Dear Al,

Poor Uncle Mike scarcely knows where to begin. First off, we need to distinguish between a) one's search for illumination, and b) one's pounding on a drum one bought in a store in hopes of invoking a romanticized male archetype.

This vision quest stuff can be tricky, Al. You really want to do your homework. If we can believe three or four millennia of testimony by an impressive and varied array of mystics, one's spiritual essence is not gender specific. Contrary to what Robert Bly might tell you, there are no girl spirits and boy spirits. After this, there's only acting out.

Moving on to the world of form, if beating drums with your fellow WASP don't-wannabes gets you off, Uncle Mike would be the last person to stand in your way. Or, for that matter, anywhere near you. Uncle Mike just hates to see full grown humans imagine that getting together once a week to evoke a scene from Dances With Wolves will somehow save the planet. Uncle Mike doubts it will even save their marriage.

As someone must have said, it's easier for the entire Sioux Nation to pass through the eye of a needle than for a marketing exec to get into heaven with his drum.

● ● ●

Dear Uncle Mike,

My wife likes to flirt and it drives me nuts. Maybe if you tell her to stop, she will.

Fed Up in Portland

Dear Fed Up,

Fat chance. In the first place, people only stop doing something when they feel like it. In the second place, Uncle Mike is a staunch defender of flirting. Libertine that he is, he regards it as the glandular counterpart to lively conversation and, like the reading of good books and the playing of good poker, he thinks it should be encouraged.

To fight flirtation is to set sail against the winds of nature since, as behaviors go, only breathing is more rampant in the animal kingdom. Uncle Mike is certain that, were we curious enough to look, we'd discover that slugs flirt, albeit very unattractively. Done well, which is to say without serious intent, flirting is about as destructive as daydreaming and much more fun than gossip. Done badly, of course, people have been shot.

If your wife makes a practice of acting the coquette and is older than 16 (something Uncle Mike prays is the case), the chance of her stopping cold turkey is one click this side of none. Maybe she does it to drive you nuts. Women do that sometimes.

Aside from the obvious heart to heart threats, Uncle Mike recommends you warn her to keep her coyness out of the workplace. Tell her that the batting of eyes leads men to daydream. Under federal guidelines, any gender specific behavior that interferes with job performance qualifies as harassment. Tell her when she's sued, you could not in good conscience be a character witness.

Dear Uncle Mike,

Is homosexuality genetically determined or is it a behavior?

Tina in Lake Oswego

Dear Tina,

In Uncle Mike's wildly unqualified opinion, yes and no. Owing to the recent discovery of variations in a small structure of the brains of homo- and heterosexual men, and to studies indicating that the ratio of hetero- to homosexuals is historically constant across cultures (about 9:1), it would seem there's some genetic hardware predisposing us to variations in dating habits.

Uncle Mike can live with this. He also believes, on the basis of personal observation, that sexual behaviors can be programmed by the software of our experience. Sexuality isn't bipolar, it's a spectrum. We all need to love and be loved. Not all love is sex, and not all sex is love, but the two are old and intimate companions.

Men and women, on the other hand, now cross the street to avoid each other. For women, sex is an act of trust and it's no longer fashionable for women to trust men, not even when the men have earned it. That men have become objects of loathing (in the good old days, we were success objects) does nothing to stoke the fires of heterosexuality. Sex without love is hollow and it's impossible to love someone you're afraid of. Women fear men physically, men fear women emotionally. Given this, Uncle Mike's not surprised to see the walking wounded of gender cleansing get together with those of like bodies to explore alternatives.

● ● ●

27

Dear Uncle Mike,
>   Does time really go faster when you're having fun?
>   Shelley in Hood River

Dear Shelley,

   It depends on what you call fun. Time slows with increased velocity so, strictly speaking (and we really should), it passes fastest when we're standing still. This explains the notion of being "happy as a clam" and the difference between fun and excitement.

   On the bright side, velocity is also linked to mass so that the faster you go, the heavier you are. Uncle Mike takes this as evidence he lives in the best of all possible worlds; a world in which, were he to jog, he would lose weight by stopping.

● ● ●

Dear Uncle Mike,

   My aunt and uncle, who I hardly know, are celebrating their 50th anniversary next month. They live an hour's drive away and our relationship is hardly a close one, just Christmas and birthday cards. The few times I've seen them as an adult, they've been aloof to both me and my husband. Are we obliged to go? Do we have to take a gift? My husband says yes but I say why be phoney? What do you think?
>   Mary R., Beaverton

Dear Mary,

The first thing you need to do is top confusing Uncle Mike with Ann Landers. At the risk of startling you, dear, there are people out there with real problems, or at least interesting ones. To say yours falls short of the mark is to hilariously understate the case.

Should you honor your blood relatives on the occasion of their golden wedding anniversary? To answer, Uncle Mike must first know if you were raised by weasels. If not, your dilemma disappears. Uncle Mike refuses even to discuss the question of gifts. If you need to ask, they probably wouldn't like what you got them.

● ● ●

Dear Uncle Mike,

I've got a guy problem. You're a guy so maybe you can help. I'm 28, single, and have a great boyfriend. Neither of us has much money but whenever we go out Peter insists on paying. In every other way, he treats me like an equal. He even let me push the car once when the battery died. Why can't I pick up a beer tab? Any ideas?
Jill W., Lincoln City

Dear Jill,

Uncle Mike's first idea is that you and he should drink beer together soon. Uncle Mike's second idea is that you might be confusing cash flow with sexual politics. Nasty mistake.

Uncle Mike loves to hear of young men bearing gifts

of food, entertainment, and beer to the women in their lives. As long as they don't imagine they're buying or leasing something in the process, it's a nice thing for them to do. As a friend, you should not discourage such acts of generosity.

Uncle Mike applauds your sense of fairness and recognizes it's important that your partner learn to receive beer as well as give it. But as any one in the barter economy, or a successful relationship, will tell you, giving takes many forms. Judging from what you cite as the only problem in your relationship, Uncle Mike would bet you give as much as you get, perhaps without knowing it.

Men are funny. If yours wants to pick up the check, practice your thank-yous. Pick the right moment, look your young swain in the eye and tell him how glad you are he's your friend.

● ● ●

Dear Uncle Mike,

My problem is my husband. After 16 years of marriage, suddenly he wants to spend time with the boys. Playing poker, shooting pool, and drinking beer. He says he deserves it. I say his place is home with his family. We have a 15-year-old daughter. Being a man, you'll probably take his side.

Donna T., McMinnville

Dear Donna,

Perhaps without meaning to, you've hurt Uncle Mike's feelings. Being more than seven in dog years, Uncle Mike has seen enough of the human comedy to shatter whatever gender loyalties or biases he suffered as a youth. He would cheerfully do volunteer work for the IRS before siding against anyone, even you, on the basis of which public restroom they use. This said, we pick up the sword of impartiality.

Your problem stems from the fact you're a neurotic control freak. Rather than confront your tacky little insecurities, you choose to make your mate's life as miserable as your own by what amounts to grounding him.

Let the poor slob out to play. What's the worst that can happen? He has a little fun? From the sound of your letter, you could use a night out yourself.

In the meantime, tell your husband for Uncle Mike that mixing the drinking of beer with the shooting of pool or the playing of poker is a horrible mistake. The only sight more pathetic than a pool player with impaired hand/ eye coordination is a poker player who feels sufficiently bullet proof to raise on a low pair after the draw.

• • •

Dear Uncle Mike,

My wife snores like a chain saw. Know any sure cures?

Wide Awake in Gresham

Dear Wide Awake,

Uncle Mike assumes you've ruled out corrective surgery. And that, in addition to acupuncture, you've explored the usual folk remedies: ritual curses, stuffing her mouth with a sock, and walling up the bedroom with pumice blocks while she sleeps. Beyond these suggestions, Uncle Mike can only pass along the method used successfully by his Aunt Moira who, possessed of a theatrical spirit when backed into the ropes, finally attacked Uncle Bub one night with a large steelhead, pounding him mercilessly about the head and chest and screaming, "I need sleep, you useless idiot." No fool, Uncle Bub took to catnapping on the porch.

● ● ●

Dear Uncle Mike,

I'm a divorced woman, 36. I'm good looking, smart, and friendly. I also haven't had a date in months. It's not that my standards are too high, Lord knows. No one's even approaching me. Is it my breath? Something I said? Other women I know are having the same problem. What's with you guys?

Cynthia S., Astoria

Dear Cynthia,

First off, Uncle Mike suggests you accept things as they are. Karma being what it is, there's a good chance you're alone for some reason. Rather than railing at the universe, admit the possibility that whatever is, is right.

It's the old Zen one liner, Cynthia: Is your life half empty or half full? Being alone is one thing, being lonely is another. In Uncle Mike's experience, folks are lonely only to the extent they define themselves as half of a pair. Although Uncle Mike will vomit if he hears even once more that a woman without a man is like a fish without a bicycle, he cautions you against imagining that a man is the antidote to some existential poison you've taken.

●●●

Dear Uncle Mike,

My girlfriend's been on me to lose a little weight. I could stand to drop maybe five pounds, but she wants me to jog with her. I think it's great if she wants to run around the neighborhood in a sweatsuit, but I'd as soon do sit-ups in front of the TV set. Is there something holy about jogging?

Dan O., Portland

Dear Dan,

Anything holy about jogging? Not to Uncle Mike. Uncle Mike makes it a rule never to run unless something large and murderous is chasing him or he's late for the meeting of his poker support group.

If you need to lose weight, pal, try eating fewer porkchops and more brown rice. If the hopeless blob of flab your friend is sure you've become could stand a little firming up, by all means do something physical. Uncle Mike recommends shuffling cards and smoking cigarettes.

Should the nagging continue, remind the love of your life of the recent Harvard study that found that men who began exercising in mid-life outlived those of us who chuckle at the thought by a startling average of ... one month. The question becomes, do you want to spend your extra month exercising?

• • •

Dear Uncle Mike,

I had my vet perform a tubal ligation on my cat last year and she's done nothing but eat ever since. Is she depressed? Should I have the good doctor untie her tubes so she can get her girlish figure back and once again attract the opposite sex? She's only 2 and the sight of her munching aimlessly on kibbles and wishing for the sound of a can opener is very sad. It's the only music she dances to anymore.

Iris B., Oregon City

Dear Iris,

First the bad news. Your vet did not perform a tubal ligation on your cat. Female humans have their tubes tied. With cats, the uterus and ovaries are surgically ripped out.

Unless you can find a kitty donor, your little dowager is as fertile now as she's ever likely to be.

So little Fluffy does nothing but eat. What, pray tell, would you have her do? Play mah jong with the girls? Is she depressed? Wouldn't you be? Aimlessly munching kibbles is at least a step up from watching talk shows and joining victim support groups. Why not get her a pet she can surgically alter? It seems to have done wonders for your grasp on reality.

●●●

Dear Uncle Mike,

After five years of marriage, my husband has decided our love life needs spicing up. I've gone along with him so far but Victoria's Secret makes me feel gift wrapped, porno flicks are silly, and power dildos just aren't my idea of fun. I'm 30, haven't led a sheltered life, and am certainly no prude, but our sex life is starting to feel like performance art instead of lovemaking. Last night he asked if I'd ever fantasized having another woman in our bed. I asked if he dreamed about singing in the Vienna Boy's Choir. Am I out of touch or is he?

Monica T., Portland

Dear Monica,

Sounds like a toss up, dear. What you're dealing with is the sexual yearnings of two incompatible agendas. That the survival of the species depends upon the coupling of psychosexual life-forms that inhabit separate cognitive universes provides much of the plot for what those still able to laugh see as the human comedy.

Your question seems to be: Is my husband becoming a sexual whacko who'll come to bed some night wearing a bunny suit and carrying a Mixmaster? One never knows, but probably not. More likely, the poor mope's just bored out of his skull. Life can do that.

If wearing lingerie as transparent as a designer's wet dream isn't your gig, tell him so. On the other hand, if you're into chenille bathrobes and sweatpants, you might give matters some thought. Does your husband put on a suit and tie when you ask? Do you think he looks handsome? Do you imagine he enjoys it with every fiber of his being?

If the naughty movies your husband brings home make you giggle till you vomit, trot out some alternatives. No matter what Andrea Dworkin says, erotica is not rape, and there must be something appealing out there since 30 percent of the adult videos, some of them probably childish, are rented by women.

As for dildos, Uncle Mike comes down foursquare on your side. He finds them horribly intimidating and, like most sexual accessorizing, unnecessary. In Uncle Mike's experience, aside from the occasional ostrich feather or riding crop, the only marital aids that deliver are flowers and fervent declarations of love. You might mention this to your husband.

You might also remind yourself neither you nor he are in this alone. If you don't like the sort of spice he comes up with, come up with some of your own. What are you saying, he's not worth the effort? Light a few candles, slip into a bubbly tub and play toesies. Then take the man to bed and burn him down. It's cheaper than marriage counseling and twice the fun.

We come now to your husband's query about company in bed. While Uncle Mike has nothing in principle against menage a trois, he doubts their utility in your situation. Tell your husband that, daydreams aside, most men are in over their heads with one woman and that adding a second will have all the therapeutic value of a divorce.

Dear Uncle Mike,

I met this really cool guy a month ago and we've been seeing each other once or twice a week since. We have a great time together, he's a lot of fun and real good looking. The only problem is he wants to have sex. I told him I need to get to know him better first. He keeps trying and getting frustrated and hurt. I get mad. Why can't guys take no for an answer?

Ready to Wait in Seaside

Dear Ready,

Why can't guys take no for an answer? They can and do, dear, every day of every miserable week of their lives. Why do they keep trying? Basically speaking, because they want to get laid and women have taught them that no's are conditional and subject to discussion.

Uncle Mike has no idea how old you are, or how long you've spent in the perfumed trenches of love, but he has a hard time believing you haven't noticed that the biological imperative that drives men is wildly different from the one that makes women prefer to walk.

No matter what Phil Donahue says, men and women are alike only to the extent that they both walk erect, breathe air, and disappoint each other. Self-help tracts and gender neutral lesson plans aren't likely to change things. Regardless how sensitive Robert Bly wannabes become, or how sexually voracious Calvin Klein models seem, testosterone isn't estrogen and it never will be.

Uncle Mike suggests you decide if this male person interests you as a love partner, then act on your decision. Anything less is a waste of time and a violation of social contract.

Letters to Uncle Mike

Dear Uncle Mike,

I'm having a recurrent dream. A large black Labrador retriever, who's actually my husband, is in my kitchen baking brownies. I pet him and he starts humping my leg. Suddenly we're in Paris. He's still a black lab, but now he has a moustache and is my waiter. I order French toast and he laughs. He brings me several small children. They're floating a foot off the ground, tethered to large red balloons. A big crow starts diving at them, popping the balloons with its beak. Now, it's raining children. I run but I can't get away. The dream always ends the same. I'm in a topless bar with Richard Gere. We're both naked, but he has a black leather collar with studs and a heart shaped dog tag. Just when he starts licking my ankles, I wake up. It's driving me nuts. Does my dream mean anything?

Donna W., Aloha

Dear Donna,

Not to Uncle Mike, but then he's not the one who needs professional help.

● ● ●

Dear Uncle Mike,

On a recent trip to Nevada, my girlfriend and I found an abandoned baby bird. We took it home and nursed it back to health. Now we find out it's a vulture. It's getting pretty big and we wonder if we should take it to the zoo or adopt it. Do vultures make good pets?

Steve S., Eugene

Dear Stupid,

In a word, no. Those who choose to live with any bird should remind themselves that all birds are linear descendants of dinosaurs. The canary's forebears were merciless, meat-eating lizards who, before they learned to fly, stood 30 feet tall and were quick as greased lightning. Being short, caged, and reduced to eating birdseed has done nothing to erase memories of the good life at the top of the food chain. Beneath the bright feathers and sweet song, your budgie is a twisted little assassin who sings only to get you close enough to the cage to render you carrion. Owing to size, their dreams usually come to nothing.

The same cannot be said of vultures. Like hawks and eagles, your vulture is a raptor, what your little lovebird would be if its prayers were answered: a large, winged carnivore with all the compassion of a cobra. Forget the Audubon specials, Steve. When push comes to shove, and it will, your buzzard will cut you no slack. As it launches itself from the armoire and shrieks down at you, its eyes flaring and talons outstretched, it will be thinking of the good old days.

Buzzard apologists will swear up and down that, given a chance, the morbid hulks are wonderful companions. This is pure hogwatch. These are the Boris Karloffs of birddom and it's no accident that nothing in the wild kingdom seeks them out. As you must have noticed, your buzzard never breaks into song. Singing is just not in them. It will never follow you around the house, chirping as you dust. What free time it has (and since buzzards are notoriously resistant to training, it will have as much as it likes) will be spent slouching on the mantle, watching your every move.

If you're at all normal, you'll tire of this. Which brings us to the only good thing that can be said of vultures: Given a good scattergun and a little determination, one can sometimes drive them off.

● ● ●

Dear Uncle Mike,

Do you think quantum mechanics is a complete description of observed reality?

Naomi M., Scappoose

Dear Naomi,

Be serious. Quantum theory fails in three fundamental ways. No, make that four.

First, quantum mechanics supplies no explanation for the quantum effect: the
appearance of a particulated something (an electron, a carrot, the Eiffel Tower) from what the equations clearly show is a background of undifferentiated and unmanifest potential. In order for there to be anything there when we look, all other possible somethings must somehow disappear, the likelihood of their existence reduced to zero by some statistical ghost in the machine. The mechanism is, as they say, unclear. Without an explanation for the rise of the universe from a mathematically pregnant nothing, quantum theory lacks a generative logic.

Second, nothing in quantum theory predicts or explains the values of the fundamental physical constants: among them, the velocity of light, the gravitational constant, Planck's quantum of least action, and the masses of the quanta. While these hubs of the phenomenal universe remain apparently random numbers, quantum theory cannot claim to be a complete description of observed reality.

Third, quantum theory is a theory of "things" observable object/events. As such, it depends upon "locality": a quality that boils down to "thisness" and "thatness." The quanta are portrayed as mass/energy islands floating on a sea of four-dimensional space/time. The separation between the islands is measured in terms of the velocity of light (an apparently random number). A strict rule of quantum mechanics (and of general relativity, the modern definition of gravity) states that nothing in the observable universe moves at a velocity greater than c, the finite speed of light. And for good reason. At velocity c, mass becomes infinite, which is to say coterminal with all that is. At velocity c, space/time becomes a construct without meaning. Without space/time, there is no separation between object/events. Without separation, there is no locality. Without locality, there is no quantum universe.

Since 1935 (see: EPR, the Einstein/Podolsky/Rosen experiment), we've had reason to suspect that something in the observable universe travels faster than light. Since 1964 (see: Bell's Connectedness Proof), we've been reasonably sure of it. All object/events in the universe seem to be linked in a relative simultaneity disallowed by the framework of quantum theory and general relativity. To paraphrase Bob Dylan, something's happening here but we don't know what it is. We do know this. Given supraliminal (faster than light) connections, the universe becomes nonlocal: a state of prephenomenal cosmic oneness in which there's no room for "things" like the quanta, let alone gaseous nebulae, Paris in the Spring, and cocker spaniels. In short, if quantum theory is correct, then quantum reality is a limited case of a deeper reality

41

about which quantum mechanics can say nothing. To call quantum theory a complete description of observed reality would be stretching the universe to its breaking point.

Finally, Naomi, there's this schizoid nature of our current paradigm. This season's model of the universe is a forced marriage of two incompatible points of view: quantum theory and general relativity. It's not just that the two theories describe two halves of the same reality. They're logically irreconcilable and mutually exclusive. In the microcosm, the world of the unimaginably small described by quantum mechanics, there's no room for anything resembling a space/time continuum. In the macrocosm, the world of the unimaginably large described by general relativity, the universe is a space/time continuum in which there's no room for particles. Observation bears out both theories and neither is in the slightest doubt. But, if one is a true picture of the universe we observe, the other is patently false. It's a pretty funny world. And one we haven't completely described yet.

●●●

Dear Uncle Mike,

After 12 years of marriage, I'm recently single. The dating game sucks. Coworkers are out and I'm too old (34) for the bar scene. I'm not into celibacy and masturbation can only take a woman so far. Here's my question. I have a longtime male friend who's also single now. We've been buddies for years, not quite brother and sister, but close. Lately, we've started flirting. Nothing overt, but the cards are there on the table, or at least I think they are. That's the problem. Should I risk our friendship and make a concrete gesture? Is being horny just making me stupid or do things like this work out?

Lonely in Eugene

Dear Lonely,

Does what work out? Making love with a friend? Rogue that he is, Uncle Mike makes it a practice never to be naked with anyone who's not.

That you sign yourself lonely is cause for concern. Uncle Mike may live alone but he's not lonely. Being lonely means never having to say you enjoy your own company. Those who don't seldom make good friends. Uncle Mike can relate all too well to the limits of celibacy and partnerless sex. But, as his granny used to say as she bounced Uncle Mike on her knee, not being involved is nature's way of saying, so what?

As to whether you should take your friend to bed, how would Uncle Mike know? If your hearts are in the right place and no one is using anyone, a roll on the futon probably won't end the friendship or the world as you know it. On the other hand, it will definitely dynamite the status quo. For the thoughtful, there's no such thing as casual sex. If what either of you is looking for is the temporarily soothing balm of an affair, Uncle Mike suggests you try the laundromat.

Should you make a gesture? What are you, new on the planet? As any man will attest, women are just as able to hit you over the head and drag you into the cave as any shell-shocked, post-Andrea Dworkin male. If your assessment is correct and the two of you are co-flirting, the poor schmuck is bound to be sweating as much blood as you. Invite him for dinner and a substantive chat. Beforehand, buy an extra toothbrush.

● ● ●

Dear Uncle Mike,
    Got a cure for the hiccups?
                              Terrie L., Maupin

Dear Terrie,
    Doesn't everyone?
    Uncle Mike was sitting on a barstool one night, watering his angst with Jack Daniels, when a nearly stunning young woman plopped down next to him. He asked how's it going, she says lousy. She's on her way to San Francisco and has been hiccuping (hiccoughing actually) since she left Seattle.
    Ever the good Samaritan, Uncle Mike asks has she's tried hanging upside down from an oak branch with a virgin badger strapped to her chest and drinking a Dr.Pepper while singing selections from Gilbert and Sullivan.
    Clearly in no mood for fun, the woman asks the barmaid for a paper napkin and a bottle of bitters. She soaks the napkin with the nasty stuff, twists it into a teat, and begins sucking on it with what can only be called studious abandon. "Works every time," she says. And, for what it's worth, that time it did.

Dear Uncle Mike,

If a tree falls in the forest and no one is there to hear it, does it make any noise?

Ralph W., Garibaldi

Dear Ralph,

Forget to take our medicine, did we Ralph? Sound, as your therapist should have explained to you, is energy made manifest as ripples in the air. Uncle Mike tries never to rain on anyone's parade, but it seems a tad egocentric to imagine that when your tympanic membranes (the little drums inside your ear) are elsewhere, the universe is reduced to miming.

Just because you aren't there doesn't mean the forest isn't. Bambi and Thumper are, we'd wager, very much aware when large tree trunks crash into the trilliums. So, for that matter, are the trees and the trilliums. One mustn't forget that plants scream when you pull them out by their roots.

On the other hand you have, perhaps without meaning to, made a point. The mother of science is empiricism: a belief system which defines reality as that, and only that, which can be measured. To measure, one must observe. Without observation, there are no events and therefore nothing we can properly call reality. In the equations of quantum mechanics, when you close your perceptions, the world goes away. Never doubt for a moment it comes back.

● ● ●

45

Letters to Uncle Mike

Dear Uncle Mike,

I feel a little stupid writing to an advice column, but here goes. My buddy's wife is coming on to me. I didn't know they were having problems but something's sure going on. Carol (not her real name) is making it pretty clear she wants to jump my bones. Dave (not his real name either) is no angel, but the idea of doing a back-door trip with his wife (who's an absolute knockout) is playing hell with my sense of ethics and loyalty. Should I do it? We're both old enough to be discreet. Should I let Dave know he's got trouble? Should I move to another town?

Tempted in Cannon Beach

Dear Tempted,

Uncle Mike sympathizes with your feelings. He feels a little silly giving advice to those who are strangers to common sense. This said, we press on.

Should you make love to your friend's wife? Gee, there's a tough one. Uncle Mike wonders which part of do-unto-others you don't understand. When your friend finds out, and he will, that the two of you regard your tawdry little urges as more important than his sanity, he's hardly going to burst into song. Ever hear of karma?

There's nothing wrong with the two of you being attracted to each other. There's nothing right about acting on it. If Not Carol is feeling lonely and unappreciated, a persistent theme of the human comedy, splitting the tab on a Motel 6 with her husband's friend probably won't be a miracle cure.

Should you say something to her? Gosh, there's a thought. Taking the moral high ground demands you douse the both of you with a bucket of cold water. Tell her the thought of making love to her makes you bite your knuckle and whimper, but that doing anything about it would be to behave in ways most often seen in alley cats.

Should you let old Not Dave know he's got trouble? If Dave is able to count to 10 and tie his own shoes, Uncle Mike would bet he has some inkling. Instead of inflicting your guilt-ridden honesty on him (Yo, Dave, I think your wife's got the hots), Uncle Mike recommends you dummy up and do your best imitation of a friend. You do this by being there for the both of them and doing it fully clothed.

Should you leave town? Absolutely. Can Uncle Mike rent your place?

●●●

Dear Uncle Mike,

I've got a problem with my boyfriend Chris. He calls me "Babe." I've told him I find it insulting. He says his father calls his mother Babe, and if she doesn't mind why should I? It's becoming a real issue. When we're making love, one "Babe" and I'm completely turned off. Any ideas?

Angie in Eugene

Dear Angie,

Uncle Mike always has ideas, some of them pretty darned clever.

Before agreeing with you that your boyfriend hasn't a leg to stand on, Uncle Mike would first attack what may be a misplaced application of politically correct gender theory. Regardless what some women might shriek as they plant their knees on your chest, your boyfriend calling you Babe doesn't necessarily make him a running dog of male oppression. What matters, cupcake, is whether or not he treats you like a full-fledged human. If he doesn't, what he calls you is the least of your worries.

This said, Uncle Mike thinks your boyfriend's behaving like a baboon. If you don't want him to call you babe, you don't want him to call you babe. To get the point across, next time you're making love, try warbling his father's name. Or, if you're feeling really nasty, his mother's.

● ● ●

Dear Uncle Mike,

My room mate and I are having an argument. Maybe you can settle it. Do octopi make good pets?

Warren T., Portland

Dear Warren,

Only for the pitifully unbalanced. Octopi are, in case you hadn't noticed, ugly beyond belief: tentacled, shell-less mollusks who, in terms of companionship, rank right up there with slugs and snails. The only bright side to octopi is how quickly they learn to fetch. You will, in fact, have a hard time stopping them. Do not, under any circumstance, let your octopus roam freely in the house. As docile and squishy as your pet seems, there'll come a day when it's feeling petulant. As your tentacled horror drags you shrieking and thrashing into its lair, you'll wish you'd listened to Uncle Mike and wrapped the aquarium with concertina wire.

● ● ●

Dear Uncle Mike,

My neighborhood in Portland, the Hawthorne District, has been taken over by yuppies and trendoids. People with more money and attitude than class crowding any sort of reality off the sidewalk. It's enough to gag a maggot. What makes my blood boil and makes me long for an assault squirt gun are the arrogant jerks who ride their thousand-dollar bicycles on the sidewalk. Is this legal? Can I do anything about it?

Cracking in Portland

Dear Cracking,

Uncle Mike shares your dismay at what things have come to. The attack of the Many Too Many (see: Designer People) has never been less pretty. Fortunately, Uncle Mike has learned that sticking his thumbs into the leaking dike of civilization makes him a dull and bitter boy with sore thumbs.

The problem boils down to vanishing manners. Like the homeless, the pretty people confuse public areas with personal space. The homeless sleep and beg there, the politically correct whine about parking, (laugh over decaf lattes like actors in chewing gum commercials), and (squeal with faux delight whenever they meet) like you, they give Uncle Mike the urge to throw up.

Is it legal for the ecologically privileged to ride their state of the art mountain bikes on the sidewalk? Probably. Can you do anything about it? Of course. Uncle Mike likes to jam a baguette into their spokes and scream, "Carpe diem!"

• • •

Dear Uncle Mike,

Could you please explain what's happening in Bosnia?

Bill T., The Dalles

Dear Bill,

Certainly. People are killing each other.

• • •

Dear Uncle Mike,

A business acquaintance of mine, a young woman in public relations, has me guessing. We have lunch every week or two and lately she's been getting "touchy." Not that I'm complaining, mind you. She's charming, intelligent, and more than attractive. The problem is that I'd hate to misjudge her intentions and ruin a business relationship. Does it mean anything when a woman pats your thigh?

Guessing in Oregon City

Dear Guessing,
   In today's world, no.

● ● ●

Dear Uncle Mike,
   I met my girlfriend on the rebound. She was just out
of a two-year relationship with a coke dealer who drove a
Firebird, smashed beer cans on his forehead and treated
her like garbage. She said I was the best thing that ever
happened to her. It's been six months now and I love her
a lot. Last month this jerk talked her into having dinner
with him. Now she sees him a couple of times a week.
She says he needs her, that he's trying to turn his life around
and she's the only one who can help him. I was understanding at first but last week I confronted her and she
admitted she slept with him, "but only once." She says
she doesn't want to lose me, but she can't abandon this
sleazeball in his time of need. This is tearing my guts up.
What should I do?
                                        Bummed Out in Portland

Dear Bummed,
   Uncle Mike wishes his problems were this simple.
You should drop her like a hot rock. What you're dealing
with is what used to be called a faithless woman. Juke-
boxes in country/western bars are filled with their stories.
And with guys drinking whiskey to forget them. If you're
feeling especially stupid and masochistic, tell her you'll
be there for her if and when she's through massaging the
hopelessly lame.

While you're being a doormat, remember that sleeping with the dysfunctional doesn't make this woman Mother Theresa. It makes her dysfunctional. As John Prine put it: "You have no complaints, you are what you are, you ain't what you ain't." The same goes for your friend. Let her work out her karma with outlaws, a not uncommon female pastime. Caution her there's a difference between outlaws and criminals. Seize the moral high ground, be a friend when you can, but keep your heart open for someone who won't eat the good parts and throw the rest away.

● ● ●

Dear Uncle Mike,

I don't know if this is up your alley or not, but my tape deck is messing up. I figured to get it repaired, but my friend the technofreak says I'm nuts, that it'll cost more to get it fixed than it would to buy a new one. I checked, and he's almost right. Then again, if I bought a new one, I'd have a new one. What would you do?

Alan R., Astoria

Dear Alan,

Even if it cost more, Uncle Mike would have his boom box repaired. Aside from showing disrespect to the wage slaves in some third world corporate sweatshop who slapped the gismotchie together, throwing it in the dumpster and buying a new one sends an inappropriate signal to the masters of disposable technology who will, given half a chance, bury us in shiny gadgets with the half-life of a summer romance. Let the swine earn an honest living.

•••

Dear Uncle Mike,
   If you had three wishes, what would they be?
                              Angela I., Portland

Dear Angela,
   Uncle Mike wants to thank you for the chance to purge his system of the demon of the half-empty cup. After winnowing down a three-page, single-spaced want list that included a 1959 TR-3 roadster, the reincarnation of his old dog Easy, a meaningless fling with Sinead O'Connor, a cedar canoe, some sort of marketable talent, a new prostate, the ability to foresee the past, the passbook interest on a million dollars, no cavities, a good banjo, a unified field equation able to be printed on a T- shirt, a woman who regards his faults as virtues, and a gig in Jamaica writing ad copy for Rastafarian retreats, Uncle · Mike feels several tons lighter. Counting your desires is every bit as therapeutic as counting your blessings, if more embarrassing.
   When pushed to the wall, Uncle Mike's three wishes would be: peace to all beings, a cabin in the coast range, and a meaningful fling with Sinead O'Connor.

Dear Uncle Mike,

I'm in my 40s and unattached. I just finished a relationship that lasted several years and ended badly. But that's not my problem. To be honest, I think it's a good time for me to be alone. I have a career, friends, and a full life. My problem is my friends. They think a man my age shouldn't be alone and persist in trying to fix me up with just about anyone. When I tell them I'm not interested, they (especially the women) think I'm hiding my real feelings and wallowing in unspoken loneliness. Nothing could be further from the truth. Any suggestions how I can get this across?

Happily Alone in Gearhart

Dear Happy,

If you're trying to get a message across, nothing beats behaving consistently. If you're not pining for love or some reasonable facsimile, it will show. So will denial, a buzzword that means not copping to reality.

Uncle Mike's no clairvoyant, but he senses you're still licking some wounds. Nothing could be more natural. While he compliments you on your ability to be alone, a rapidly vanishing talent, he wonders if you might not be whistling Dixie. Your women friends probably have your best interests at heart and could be right. You might need a new love.

Uncle Mike recommends you meet these new women. If they interest you, carve out the sort of relationship you want. Lay your cards on the table. Let them know you've taken a vow of abstinence until you've plumbed the depths of the human heart.

● ● ●

Dear Uncle Mike,

Ever since I took my 8-year-old daughter to see Jurassic Park, she's been wanting a baby alligator. Do they make good pets?

Laura S., Beaverton

Dear Laura,

Uncle Mike hesitates to believe you're serious. Explain to your daughter that Steven Spielberg's dinosaurs were pretend. Alligators are real in ways that are horribly unpleasant. Being reptiles, alligators divide the world into two parts: that which should be killed and eaten and that which should only be killed. When she whines that her alligator will only be a baby, tell her this only makes the little psychotic quicker on its feet. Your daughter must look truth in the face. Cuddling is a concept that's eluded alligators for hundreds of million of years and play is something they don't even do with their food.

● ● ●

Dear Uncle Mike,

Are you pro-life or pro-choice?

Angela W., Roseburg

Dear Angela,

Before answering, Uncle Mike would like to point out it's none of your business. But if you're rude enough to ask, Uncle Mike is polite enough to respond. After much searching of his soul, Uncle Mike's decided he's both.

Pro-life? Who isn't? Not only is Uncle Mike all for life, he can't imagine it's something he or anyone else can stop.

A growing mountain of evidence indicates the universe itself is alive. Is a fetus alive? Of course, from the half of forever that came before its conception through the half of forever that follows it. There's no room in the equations of quantum physics for death, only for the dissolution of integral systems.

Speaking of integral systems, Uncle Mike figures that whatever's inside your body is yours, a notion that includes both urine specimens and unborn progeny. This makes him devoutly pro-choice. Once again, who could not be? A day without choice is a day without free will, one of the few things worth dying to prevent.

A woman who decides, for any reason, to abort her unborn child is not being anti-prolife, she's simply yielding to the truth that, for whatever reason, she's unable to meet the demands of raising a new human being. Given the results of bad parenting displayed on the nightly news and in a shopping mall near you, this decision hardly qualifies as immoral.

Finally, Uncle Mike is bothered by the attitude that human life is more sacred than any other. Uncle Mike wonders if those milling angrily in front of Planned Parenthood clinics eat meat, support the slaughter of strangers in war, or have any adopted children.

● ● ●

Dear Uncle Mike,

I'm 23 and my boyfriend and I have been living together for about a year. He wants to get married. I'm not so sure. I know I love him, but I don't know if I know enough to know I want to make that kind of commitment. Is everyone this uncertain? My mom reads you, so I figure you're older and might have some good advice.

Cold Feet in Newport

Dear Cold Feet,

Your hunch is right. Uncle Mike is older than you. Much older and deliriously happy about it. He did youth once and, though it was ever so much fun, it tired him badly.

Is everyone uncertain? Only if they have more brains than the average crowbar. People who are certain about things are not only dangerous but make poor dinner companions. Is everyone uncertain about marriage? Aside from characters in poorly crafted fiction, yes. And for excellent reason.

Marriage is an oath, eventually sealed in blood, between two people to love, honor, and cherish each other until one or both of them croak. Marriage is a vow of friendship taken in the unseen face of eating and sleeping with each other for, say, fifty years. Marriage means putting another human's interests on a level equal to your own and maintaining this posture for better or for worse, a phrase that takes on startling new meaning after a decade or two.

Having been married once, Uncle Mike is now happily unattached, but wouldn't have missed a minute of the insanity, hysteria, and mind-numbing ennui of pair-bonding. Does Uncle Mike have advice for you? No, just an observation. Given love, patience, a healthy

57

respect for change, and the knowledge we learn more from our mistakes than we do from our successes, marriage isn't any trickier than the rest of life.

●●●

Dear Uncle Mike,
    Does time end?

                   Nervous in Portland

Dear Nervous,
    Uncle Mike loves questions that get right to the point and is beside himself at the chance to forget the human comedy for a moment to consider simple things like quantum cosmology.

    Let's begin our meditation with Einstein's mantra: no space, no time, only space/time. Space and time are the warp and woof of the universe, elements of its geometry, as inseparable as the circumference and diameter of a sphere. Time doesn't flow through space, object/events occur in space/time. Does time have a stop? Yes, but just before it happens, your watch will slow to the point that a second will take the rest of forever to pass.

    Here's the thing. By the rules of general relativity, mass increases with velocity. At the velocity of light, mass becomes infinite and space/time disappears; or rather, becomes a term without meaningful referents. An object/event possessing infinite mass would be, by definition, equal to all that is. The only object/event with possibly infinite mass is the universe. At the velocity of light, the particular and the general are one. There is no difference, without difference no motion, and without motion no space/time.

You ask does this ever happen? Theoretically speaking, neither quantum theory nor its partner in paradigm, general relativity, rule it out. Where would it happen? Two places: the event horizon surrounding black holes and the outer edge (itself a meaningless term) of the universe. Let's work from the outside in.

The Doppler effect, one of the cornerstones of observational physics, defines the inverse relationship between velocity and frequency. Imagine a series of waves. Make them go faster and they stretch out. By measuring the stretch, we're able to tell how fast galaxies are moving and in which direction. They are, basically speaking, moving away from us. (If it's any consolation, it looks that way from any point in the universe.) Here's the fun part. The further away the galaxy is, the faster it's going. Galaxies at the very edge of the observable universe are traveling at velocities approaching that of light. In theory, there is nothing to stop their velocity from increasing. Hold that thought while we look at black holes.

Gravitation is a warping of the fabric of space/time. Black holes are gravitational warps so profound that not even light can escape them. Whole galaxies fall into them like sand into a funnel. The closer they get, the faster they go. We'll never see a black hole because, quite literally, there's nothing to see. We can only observe their effects. The surface of a black hole has an interesting name: the event horizon. It's called this because, as bits of mass are accelerated to the velocity of light, they disappear into the black hole's undifferentiated inertia. There's something very poignant about this. Black holes are surrounded by a halo of radiation: the electromagnetic

59

shriek mass/energy makes when it's torn apart by unimaginable gravitational forces. Even when you call it decoupling, it's sad.

Uncle Mike hears you. What happens next? A big fat nothing. Inside a black hole, there is no difference. That's why not even light can escape. Without difference, nothing happens. The same must hold true outside the interior surface of the universal sphere. When those galaxies hit escape velocity, they disappear, babe. But, like Uncle Mike said, from your perspective, you'll never get there. Time slows with velocity and crossing that last meter to the event horizon will take you the next half of forever. Like many things in life, waiting for it as fast as you can doesn't guarantee it'll ever come.

● ● ●

Dear Uncle Mike,

My apartment doesn't allow cats. Do fish make good pets?

Lonely in Bend

Dear Lonely,

Uncle Mike has no idea how lonely you are but he has difficulty imagining a fish would be much help. Anyone who tells you fish have personalities are either not normal or fooling themselves. Unless your fish is a hammerhead shark, and it really shouldn't be, it will be less fascinating than a lava lamp. When it comes to companionship, fish rank next to rocks. Regardless how tough your day has been, or how much you need a friend, your guppy will never be there with a shoulder to cry on. There's a good chance it won't even know you're there.

●●●

Dear Uncle Mike,

My girlfriend dumped me a while back and I can't seem to let it go. I'm fine for awhile then somebody mentions her name or I run into her on the street and I choke up. Usually, for me, when it's over it's over. This time it's different. Any tips for curing a broken heart?

Mopey in Tigard

Dear Mopey,

Dozens. For starters, you could find another woman. There's much to be said for the curative powers of spending time with someone who's not tired of you yet. Failing this (and, given your moping, this could easily happen), cop to the fact you're mentally unhinged. Not because you're shuffling around in your bathrobe asking Shakespearian questions of the universe. We all do that. You're unbalanced because you're living in the past.

Listen Hamlet, the woman you love isn't just gone, she no longer exists as anything more than a selective memory you're evoking to emotionally disembowel yourself. Aside from this unholy ghost, it sounds like what you're in love with is being in love. Good for you. Just don't imagine it excuses you from rational thought. As Uncle Mike learned from diagramming sentences, to have a subject you need an object.

Love, or at least the portions of it we can observe, is a whirlpool of emotions in a sea of space/time whose wave pattern isn't the same even once. Can you dig it? What the two of you experienced, and Uncle Mike doesn't doubt for a moment it was the stuff epics are made of, was a phase interaction between two spiritual waveforms masquerading as humans with separate agendas.

Just like real life, love depends on who we are, where we're going, and what time it is. Paths fork, things happen, people change. She's no longer who she was, neither are you, and the home your heart's trying to get back to has been bulldozed to make way for a shopping mall.

● ● ●

Dear Uncle Mike,
What do you think of the Tonya Harding affair?
Tracy M., Astoria

Dear Tracy,
As little as possible.

● ● ●

Dear Uncle Mike,
I met the perfect man. Unfortunately, he's married. Our work throws us together and we've had lunch and dinner several times. Neither of us has made a first move.

He's a perfect gentleman but I can feel the tension building. Neither of us are kids. I've never had an affair with a married man but, thought I know things could turn out badly, I'm sorely tempted. What do you think?

Ready for Love in Lake Oswego

Dear Ready For a Big Mistake,

Uncle Mike thinks you're about to learn one of the more spectacular lessons of life. Haven't we seen this movie before, munchkin? The afternoons of gay abandon, the taste of stolen fruit, the thrill of betrayal, the flush of dishonesty and guilt, the giddy freedom of violating your principles and sucker punching innocent bystanders.

At the risk of being corny, Uncle Mike would remind you of the golden rule. You remember, do unto others? That one? If you were married to this man, would you mind if he had a fling? Bring you closer together would it? Build your character? Or gut your faith?

To paraphrase Thumper, if you can't do something nice, don't do nothing at all. Whether you believe in karma or not, it exists, has large wheels and grinds exceedingly fine. Trust Uncle Mike, poops. Once the bloom wears off your tawdry little romp, the fun will never start.

In closing, Uncle Mike would like to congratulate you on discovering the perfect man and urges you to contact the Smithsonian. There may be a prize.

●●●

63

Letters to Uncle Mike

Dear Uncle Mike,

I just tested HIV positive. To put it mildly, I'm a little down. I know it's not a death sentence, I might never develop AIDS, they might find a cure, God could ride over the hill in a Buick convertible, but I'm thinking about mortality. Any cheery thoughts about death and dying?

Marty in Portland

Dear Marty,

Owing to his loose tether on reality, Uncle Mike has cheery thoughts about almost everything. He is, for instance, wildly upbeat about your budding interest in mortality. We should all spend our time so well.

First off, the new age mantra, "Today is the first day of the rest of your life," is naked twaddle. Uncle Mike wakes each morning with a chirp on his lips and the solid knowledge this could be his last day on the planet. This doesn't make Uncle Mike morbid. It makes him plan his time more wisely than he otherwise might. As someone once pointed out, no one lying on their death bed ever wished they'd spent more time at the office.

As for death per se (see: Grim Reaper, Big Casino, and Sinners in the Hands of An Angry God), having seen no evidence of it in nature, Uncle Mike finds death a silly notion to embrace. He suspects it's promoted by those with something to gain from scaring people.

No, in denying death, Uncle Mike isn't slipping into hot tub metaphysics. It's a fact of life that all systems decay (see: Entropy, Thermodynamics, and Wrinkles). Uncle Mike has no quarrel with accepting that large systems, our bodies among them, will ultimately (and at just the right moment) fling off their pattern integrities and dissolve into smaller, simpler, and perhaps cuter systems. In fact, after a tumbler of sour mash whiskey, he finds it charming.

In terms of the physical universe and our awareness of it, this transformation of macro to micro system is the only "passing on" that "death" can refer to. Breathtaking as this mass/energy imperative might be, Uncle Mike sees a big difference between the transmutation of vibrating nothingness (see: Quantum Wave Mechanics) and being a) cast into a fiery furnace, or b) lofted to a cloud draped Oz where one can eat bonbons without gaining weight.

Moving from the physical to the metaphysical, death still remains a term without meaningful referents. Uncle Mike is just a country boy but, being a born again Pythagorean (see: As Above, So Below and Universe as Number), he regards himself as more concept than demonstrable fact. To be honest, Uncle Mike sees himself as a spiritual waveform at play, forever, in the fields of space/time. Then again, Uncle Mike also collects bits of bright colored yarn.

To Uncle Mike, Uncle Mike is a point-conscious perspective of the four dimensional geometry of being (see: General Relativity, Von Neumann's Proof, and Siddhartha), no more distinct than a teardrop in the ocean of possibility (see: Bell's Interconnectedness Theorem and the Collapse of Quantum Probabilities). Nonempirical heretic that he is, Uncle Mike believes he's a discrete frequency of that light they talk about in Genesis, neither holy nor dispensable.

Worries about his prostate aside, Uncle Mike's universe is a moveable feast at which he's both host and guest. Temporal existence is a joke played on the Specific by the General (see: Velocity of Light and the Principle of Locality), and Uncle Mike sees no reason not to believe he hasn't always been here. In a closed and unbounded universe, he has nowhere to go and would probably stay home and watch his lava lamp anyway.

Letters to Uncle Mike

Dear Uncle Mike,

What do you think about a 45-year-old woman who's seeing a 24-year-old man?

George S., Eugene

Dear George,

That the two of them have much to learn and that, if no one interrupts them, it shouldn't take long.

● ● ●

Dear Uncle Mike,

The neighbor's 10-year-old boy sits in his upstairs window and sneaks peeks at my 12-year-old daughter. My husband says it's normal behavior and he'll outgrow it. I'm thinking to bounce the little jerk off the sidewalk. What do you say?

Jenny in Lincoln City

Dear Jenny,

While Uncle Mike understands how satisfying it would be to, shall we say, impress upon the lad the principle of action and consequence, he advises you to think long and hard before dropkicking the little thrill sneak. Ten-year-olds come with lawyers these days.

And you mustn't discount the possibility your husband's right. The child may be a victim of his hormones, a clear case of testosterone-induced insanity that will disappear naturally from the palette of his behavior.

Then again, so what? Uncle Mike believes in seeing things as they are. The kid's a peeping Tom. If it were Uncle Mike's 12-year-old daughter whose privacy was being molested, he'd rent a floodlight and blind the little pervert.

● ● ●

Dear Uncle Mike,

My name is Kevin. I am 10-years old. My mom and dad told me to write to you so I am. They make me go to bed at ten o'clock even on weekends. My friends don't have to. Do you think this is fair? They said they'd listen to you.

Kevin M., Corvallis

P.S. Are you a real person?

Dear Kevin,

Is Uncle Mike a real person? Think for a moment, Kevin. If he weren't, would a clever lad like yourself be writing to him? Of course not. So you go to bed at ten o'clock. Good for you. Humans your age need lots of rest because soon, as a teenage mutant ninja pleasure sloth, you'll be up all night popping pimples and joy riding with your hormones. Are your parents fascist swine for setting an early bedtime? No. Just bigger and smarter than you.

● ● ●

Dear Uncle Mike,

What exactly are your credentials for dispensing free advice?

Allison D., Newport

Dear Allison,

Uncle Mike has, small surprise, been asked this question before. And in much the same spirit of rancor and distrust. Your suspicions are right on the mark. Uncle Mike is deliriously bereft of any credentials in counseling. Centuries ago when he was in college, he observed that the study of psychology attracts those most urgently in need of its professional services. He opted instead to study literature, a field in which the aberrant is at least elevated to art.

You shouldn't confuse Uncle Mike's confession with apology. Being sharp as a tack and more than seven in dog years, Uncle Mike feels every bit as able as Ann Landers to comment on the slapstick lunacy of life. He is, however, superficially wounded by your reference to "free advice." Uncle Mike is paid for his services, thank you very much. It may not be much, but it does help defray the cost of his visiting nurse.

●●●

Dear Uncle Mike,

My girlfriend and I moved in together a few months ago. Things were great until she got a kitten. Suddenly, I'm chopped liver. She pays more attention to "Kissy" than she does to me. Is it crazy to be jealous over a cat? Isn't it way weird to be more affectionate to an animal than you are to your lover?

Spurned in Tillamook

Dear Spurned,

Uncle Mike must hedge his bet on the grounds of insufficient data. Knowing neither you nor Kissy, it's difficult to judge which one of you your friend should put out at night. On now to your burning problem.

Is it crazy to be jealous over a cat? Interesting word, crazy. Like many behavioral accoutrements of love, jealousy is several clicks the other side of rational behavior. Ownership of another human is illegal, to say nothing of impossible. Still, we persist. Being no stranger to such psychotic breaks, Uncle Mike can only point out that after he's indulged himself, he feels lower than worm droppings.

But we were talking about you. This much is certain: It's time for you and your sweet baboo to sit down for a substantive chat. Explain very calmly that you're feeling displaced, that you think she holds Kissy in higher regard than she holds you. She'll laugh and deny it and call you a moron. And that will be that. Trust Uncle Mike, she'll never, never give up her feelings for her cat and asking her to choose between the two of you will be the most humiliating experience of your life.

Things needn't be hopeless. Uncle Mike suggests you get a dog. Not only will "Sparky" love you and your ramshackle little neuroses with an embarrassing lack of restraint, but your paranoid plots against Kissy will only deepen his loyalty.

● ● ●

Letters to Uncle Mike

Dear Uncle Mike,

Last week, my husband of fifteen years went out for drinks after work with his buddies and they wound up at a topless bar. I'm furious. He says I'm making a big deal of nothing. I say if he wants to look at a naked woman, he should come home. Who's off base here?

Forty and Furious, Cannon Beach

Dear Foaming At The Mouth,

Uncle Mike would call it a tie. First off, your husband is a fullblown nitwit to have told you. After fifteen years, he should have known better than to think you'd file his little adventure in the land of koochie-koochie under the heading of meaningless larks. In Uncle Mike's experience, wives and girlfriends see nothing meaningless about naked young women. What they see is betrayal. What they feel is disgust, outrage, and justification for violence. Most men smart enough to make change know this by the time they're old enough to get into a nudie bar.

One way or another, your husband is special. He's either honest to a fault or too stupid to worry about. Don't go upside his head with a skillet. Give the man the benefit of the doubt. Maybe his friends dragged him into the place under protest and he sat the whole time with his back to the stage. Maybe he watched the ballgame on tv. It could happen. Of course, it didn't, so if he runs any of this nonsense by you, go upside his head with a skillet.

The crucial thing is that you not lose your sense of proportion. Uncle Mike knows you won't believe this but your husband's appreciative viewing of naked dancing girls was not, and will never be, a hostile act directed against you. You were, there's no delicate way to put this, the furthest thing from his mind. That he admired the young women's work doesn't mean he'd race off at the drop of a g-string for a wild weekend in Winnemucca. As Art Crum put it so well, it don't mean nothing, Mr. Natural.

Men, bless their little stimulus/response software, like to look at pretty women. They especially like it when the pretty women are naked and pretend to flirt with them. Inveterate old dog that he is, Uncle Mike sees nothing evil in this. As with most of the human comedy, the critical factor is attitude. Few sights in the world are more amazing than a middle-aged drunk in a nude bar who honestly believes the sweet young thing taking his dollars is dancing just for him. Only you would know if your husband is that stupid.

●●●

Dear Uncle Mike,
    Which drug do you think is the more dangerous, marijuana or alcohol?
                              Marlene W., Beaverton

Dear Marlene,
    On the advice of his lawyer and his day nurse, Uncle Mike must first deny any personal knowledge of controlled substances that grow out of the ground in front of God and everyone. This said, Uncle Mike must laugh and laugh.
    In his decades of experience with Tennessee sour mash whiskey, Uncle Mike has learned that the decisions he makes and the behavior he exhibits while being God's

own drunk are leagues behind those he forgets to when he's stoned. If he'd ever been stoned, which he never ever has.

Say what you will about dipping potato chips in chocolate syrup and watching a lava lamp, it's a whole lot more in touch with reality than driving home when you can't walk, or unraveling the story of your life to someone who wishes you'd move down a stool.

As for dangerous drugs, here's Uncle Mike's short list: money, gasoline, and television.

● ● ●

Dear Uncle Mike,

My girlfriend rags on me because I won't eat lobster. I say the things are too ugly to put in your mouth. She says I have no class. What do you think?

Dave S., Coos Bay

Dear Dave,

Uncle Mike thinks he's reached the bottom of his mail bag. Not knowing you, and you mustn't confuse this with a desire to, Uncle Mike can't in good faith disagree with your friend. You may be, in fact, absolutely bereft of class. For all Uncle Mike knows, you're gauche and outré. But your refusal to eat lobster hardly makes the case. Given a choice between eating underwater insects and going hungry, Uncle Mike would cheerfully gnaw bark from trees.

Dear Uncle Mike,

About a month ago, I met this great woman through mutual friends. We hit it off right away and see each other now once or twice a week. She's intelligent, beautiful, caring, and has a great sense of humor. I can't remember a woman whose company I've enjoyed more. So what's the problem? I'm 45, she's 26, I'm white, she's African American. None of our evenings have ended over breakfast yet, but it's obvious we're both thinking about it. Neither of us are into casual flings or are unaware of the difficulties involved. Any thoughts?

Smitten in Seattle

Dear Smitten,

Uncle Mike has many thoughts. That's why he's Uncle Mike. You mention difficulties. That the two of you emerged from separate gene pools or that the woman is young enough to be your niece? Uncle Mike sees them both as confusion factors.

In the first place, applying reason to affairs of the heart is irrational. Worse, it's dog dumb. Love is hard enough to come by in this world without imposing sanctions on who gets to love whom. At 45, you should be sufficiently dry behind the ears to know that the part of us that falls in love is the spirit. The nice thing about spirits is they lack age, race, or gender.

So much for the greeting card claptrap and on to real life. Difficulties, cupcake? Uncle Mike wonders if you have any idea. He won't bother to mention the near certain outbreak of heart attack and stroke in both families. Make no mistake, boy-o, there'll be wailing in the tents. This need not nor should not deter you. Humans have a great capacity for accepting what they can't change, even if it means having a middle-aged honky in the woodpile.

By now, the two of you should be used to being stared at. The success of "Roots" and "'I'll Fly Away" not withstanding, interracial coupling is still an oddity, bringing with it all the privilege and respect you'd expect ·from a society that mass produces "Dare To Be Different" t-shirts and fails to see the joke. The important thing is to make sure you're not in love with the idea of being in love with a black woman. In that direction lies nothing but pain and sadness.

Though more subtle than issues of race, your age difference will make matters at least as problematic. To her friends, most of whom weren't born when you registered for the draft, you'll be an old geek who should be ashamed of himself. To your friends, most of whom have children her age, you'll be an old fool who should have his head examined. What they dismiss as youthful folly on her part, they'll see as a character flaw in you, one with tragedy written all over it. They will, in short, fear you're falling apart.

To all of which, Uncle Mike makes rude noises with his armpit. If you care about this woman and she cares about you, you owe each other a dance. In Uncle Mike's opinion, the most serious challenge you face is the one that faces all of us: men and women inhabit separate perceptual/conceptual universes. Uncle Mike refuses even to get started on that one.

● ● ●

Dear Uncle Mike,

This is a little embarrassing, but here goes. I hear my women friends complaining that all their boyfriends want to do is have sex. I should be so afflicted. My boyfriend and I have been living together for a little over a year and, to him, anything more than twice a week qualifies as wanton abandon. We're both in our early thirties and, other than libidos, we're a great match. Unfortunately, good and frequent sex is important to me and I'm starting to have real second thoughts about our future. Worse, I'm obsessing. You're a guy. Is this something he'll get over? Would counseling help?

Annie S., Portland

Dear Annie,

Would counseling help? Maybe. Is your boyfriend's lack of the want-to's something he'll get over? How would Uncle Mike know? He's never met either of you.

Uncle Mike assumes your boyfriend lacks valid reasons for his ennui; that, since moving in with him, you've not turned into a nagging slattern in a mumu who only stops shrieking and bearing grudges long enough to open a new box of bonbons. Uncle Mike also assumes you've tried the usual Pavlovian encouragements: candlelit bubblebaths, vegetable oil wrestling, ostrich feathers, the Little BoPeep outfit. Uncle Mike further assumes you've taken your little woodchuck aside, explained the level of your frustration and discontent, and made plain the many consequences awaiting him should he continue to neglect what is to you the bellow of Mother Nature.

If he fails to respond to any of these whistles, you've got a dog that's just not going to hunt. This leaves you three options. The first is to embark on the sort of sexual relationship that doesn't involve a second person. The second, nearly as popular, involves out of town trips with attentive men who, with your eyes closed, resemble Clint

Eastwood. The third is to leave the hopeless mope and have drinks with Uncle Mike.

●●●

Dear Uncle Mike,

You're a guy, maybe you can answer me this. Why is it a guy says he's going to call you and doesn't and that's okay, but if you don't call him he lays a guilt trip on you? Is this a guy thing? Is there a cure?

Erika in Portland

Dear Erika,

From your question and its sentence structure, Uncle Mike assumes you're fairly new on the planet. Of the many gender specific plot lines of the human comedy, the laying on of guilt is not one of them. Uncle Mike learned guilt on his mother's knee and, popular psychology tracts aside, he regards it as one of the great motivators of life, second only to fear. Or is it lust? Ah well, no matter.

The importance of guilt in mating has been impressed on Uncle Mike time and again by the various lovely women who've bunny-hopped across his self esteem. The technique is both simple and older than dirt: convince someone who cares that they've wronged and hurt you by some nebulous act or non-act which, if they really loved you, they'd recognize and understand), and they'll spend the rest of their natural life trying vainly to make up for it.

Is there a cure for guilt? Only if there's a willing patient. Those into guilt trips fall into two groups: those who know what they're doing and those who don't. Those who don't understand are more responsive to reasoning and naked threat but are often so clueless about life in general as to make them scarcely worth retraining. Those who jolly well know what they're doing are not, for the most part, about to stop. Why should they, given the bumper crop of schmucks more than willing to roll over and put their paws in the air on the off chance someone will rub their tummy?

As with most of the amusing messes we make of our lives, the solution only seems to involve a second party. Disengagement is always an option. So your sweet baboo is shoveling guilt? Tell the mindless jerk you're up to here with his neurosis and if he wants to play victim he can find a new sand box. Then feel guilty if you don't walk your talk.

● ● ●

Dear Uncle Mike,
My ten-year-old daughter has developed an interest in spiders. It started as a school project. We supported her interest and now she wants a tarantula in her room. Is this normal?
Squeamish in Warrenton

Dear Squeamish,
By Uncle Mike's standards, no. Spiders are one of nature's nightmares and those who do anything but avoid them are pitifully unbalanced. You should not, under any circumstance, allow your little deviant to bring a tarantula into your home. She'll promise to keep it in its little terrarium with a brick on the lid. She'll be lying. She'll eventually confuse her large mandibled arachnid

with a pet who knows which side its bread is buttered on, or so much as cares. Trust Uncle Mike: as sure as God made little green apples, the morning will come when, before you've had your first cup of coffee, her blank-eyed wooly horror will scurry out from under the refrigerator and leap onto your face. Statistics show you'll not be able to squoosh it fast enough.

● ● ●

Dear Uncle Mike,

I'm sure you've heard this one before. My husband and I have been married for sixteen years. There's not much love left. He goes to work, he comes home, I feed him, he sits on the couch, watches television, ignores our two children (ten and fourteen), and goes to bed. Don't even ask about lovemaking. I'm staying with him for the kids and because my job skills are limited. Do you think I'm an idiot?

Marge in Seattle

Dear Marge,

Yes. On Uncle Mike's block, a marriage like yours is called a dead horse. Any cowgirl with the brains God gave a two-by-four finds a new horse and rides quickly out of Dodge.

No, Uncle Mike's not ignoring the difficulties involved. Sixteen years of inertia masquerading as love, honor, and duty is a tough act to follow, but staying together for the kids is not always the act of a responsible adult. One parent at peace is worth two parents at war. One parent busy living is worth two parents busy pretending. As for security, the benefits of comfort in a pressure cooker of unrequited needs are nothing compared to clipping coupons in an apartment free of emotional suffocation.

Uncle Mike assumes you've talked this over with your dead horse until you're blue in the face. Make one last effort to revive it, remembering if you can what you loved about this lout to begin with. Encourage him to do the same. While you're wasting time, upgrade your job skills and, in a ladylike manner, acknowledge the smiles of attentive men.

● ● ●

Dear Uncle Mike,
I'm not sure, but I think my girlfriend's cheating on me. How do you know if a woman's having an affair?
Dennis M., Portland

Dear Dennis,
Not knowing how clueless you are, it's a challenge knowing where to begin. A good first step would be to ask her. If she tells you you're out of your mind, you've probably got trouble.

Here's Uncle Mike's checklist: Has she begun to hum for no reason? Does she stare at you, shake her head, and sigh? Is she suddenly curious about what you'd look like with a moustache? Has she manifested new concern for your happiness and personal growth? Has the phrase "follow your bliss" snuck into her conversations? Does she, at crucial moments, cry out someone else's name?

Dear Uncle Mike,

Since you've got a half-baked opinion on everything else, what are your thoughts on O.J. Simpson?

Michelle S., Seattle

Dear Snotty,

On the basis of having watched none of the televised saga or suffered through a single column inch of its fevered analysis in the much too popular press, Uncle Mike has reached a fully baked conclusion. Since he doesn't know these people and he wasn't there, it's none of Uncle Mike's business.

● ● ●

Dear Uncle Mike,

I'm a 26-year-old woman—single, intelligent, warm, caring, reasonably attractive, sensual, and often charming. Here's my question. Where are all the good men? All I get is whiners, slackers, and aging adolescents without a car, gas money, ambition, or a clue. I don't think I'm all that picky, but I'm not desperate enough to caretake cynics whose cup is always half empty, put BandAids on the knees of skateboarders old enough to in graduate school, or support lovers who sleep around. Any suggestions, Answer Man?

Selective Shopper in Seattle

Dear Selective Shopper,

Uncle Mike's first suggestion is that you change your mating metaphor before he gags. One shops for clothing, new draperies, fresh produce or, in Uncle Mike's case, the perfect Spanish coffee. Shopping for a human being ended, ostensibly at least, with the Civil War.

Since you describe yourself as intelligent, Uncle Mike hesitates to suggest the obvious: that you're shopping for love in the wrong places. Fishing, as it were, in the wrong holes. Lacking the vaguest notion of what you consider a good man, though he does have a horrible idea, Uncle Mike would be hard pressed to list likely venues. As an alternative, he suggests you stop shopping altogether. Unlike finding the best cellular phone service, finding love is more often a wonderful accident than the result of clear-eyed product research.

On the hopeful side, Uncle Mike can't help but notice many of the male traits you find loathsome and beneath you are age specific. Here Uncle Mike must sympathize. Having been a young man himself once, Uncle Mike has nothing but compassion for the young women who try to make something of them. Pet rocks are easier to train and, in many cases, better company. You might consider an older man. Someone with the experience to be amused by women, young and old, who in their search for the perfect man they so richly deserve, price themselves out of the market. Please don't let Uncle Mike know how it works out.

● ● ●

Dear Uncle Mike,
        Does humanity have a future?
                        Concerned in Cannon Beach

Dear Concerned,

Interesting word, future. A little silly in the face of mounting evidence that the universe exists as a simultaneous mass/energy gestalt, a space/time continuum of unbroken and infinite nowness in which yesterday and tomorrow are relative responses to a poorly framed question, but interesting nonetheless. Does humanity have a future? We have yet to prove it has a past and neither of them matter unless you count time; which, at bottom, our universe apparently doesn't.

The principles of quantum/relativistic reality aside, Uncle Mike can dig where you're coming from. What with holes in the ozone layer, vanishing salmon, sexually transmitted immunological plagues, Bosnia, and Rush Limbaugh, the human comedy isn't all that funny these days. One could, of course, make a case it never has been. As lifeforms go, and they all eventually do, ours has a pronounced penchant for psychotic behavior. The seven deadly sins were not, after all, discovered by observing other species and Holy Crusades were every bit as unamusing as the Holocaust. Our current psychosis involves imagining we're separate from nature. Pretty funny stuff.

If humanity has a future, Uncle Mike has serious doubts it lies in the hands of government by global corporations for whom business as usual is an obscene coupling of power and profit whose only goal is the sanctification of greed. At its present stage of evolution at least, the corporation has allegiance to nothing but self interest. Corporations live nowhere, have no sense of place, no loyalty to anything but positive cash flow. In order to feel good about itself, it must rape the planet, defecate where the rest of us eat, and steal anything not nailed down by international trade agreements they draft themselves. If global corporations were humans, they'd be hunted down and beaten with large sticks.

Uncle Mike's faith, and he still has a great deal, lies with the peasants and the notion of critical mass. Chain reactions, the point at which processes become self generating, are not restricted to nuclear power plants. Humanity is the sum of individual acts. When 51 percent of us practice right thought and right action, matters will change for the better. They'll not change one minute sooner. Why would they?

● ● ●

Dear Uncle Mike,

I'm an easygoing woman but I can be backed into a corner. I've had it up to here with stupid answering machine messages that sacrifice brevity for cleverness or are delivered by children whose parents find them cute. Knowing you, you have some withering countermeasure to suggest. Care to share it?

Shirley H., Coloma, CA

Dear Shirley,

Eventually, yes. First, Uncle Mike would like to know how someone in Coloma, California found Uncle Mike in Cannon Beach. For reasons we needn't go into, it makes Uncle Mike nervous to be found by anyone too distant to loan him money or buy him a drink.

He would also point out that the name of your town sounds awfully like a tumor.

As for answering machine messages which, in a kinder and gentler society, would constitute grounds for public flogging, Uncle Mike waits for the beep before flooding his instrument with unfortunate sounds from his tuba.

● ● ●

Dear Uncle Mike,

I read somewhere that cellular phones cause brain tumors. Do you know anything about this?

Eric in Coos Bay

Dear Eric,

Uncle Mike knows everything. Why else would he be filling in for Ann Landers while she's in rehab?

While Uncle Mike is a great fan of technology and can't imagine life without his lava lamp, he must question the wisdom of bombarding delicate neural tissue with narrow beam microwave radiation. For every action, a reaction. In this case, it's one that can bake a potato in ten minutes. Do cellular phones cause brain tumors? Judging from the boorish, self-important behavior of those who use them, Uncle Mike refuses to rule it out. The next growth industry should be diversion programs for those with an inordinate fear of being out of touch.

● ● ●

Dear Uncle Mike,

Is there anything you could find out that would make you wish to stop living? Is there anything or anyone you cannot live without?

I am so sad. I feel bereft, spiritually. I feel like I am not real enough, like life is always such a compromise. I know you'd have to be an idiot in this day and age to not feel that, but I feel like I am meant to feel something strong and good. I feel like I will someday. I used to, actually. It was a feeling that I thought I'd be able, someday, to   actualize and insulate, to make strong. It was my goal for adulthood.

I assumed there'd be someone else, an S.O. (that's PC speak for significant other) who'd fit into the picture. But it's not just a relationship, it's a whole thing. And it's not instant and constant and easy, simple, reassuring like it used to be. It comes and goes. Sometimes I want it to go away. I call it (snidely) Erikaland, after my name.

Um, it has to do with my place in the world. Why do I feel so ineffectual? Why do I care? I just do. Am I an egomaniac? Headed for disaster? Disappointment? Yawn, I'm getting sleepy. I've also lost my ability to dream, and even (this is embarrassing) my ability to fantasize sexually. This has never been an issue with me. I think I feel unlovable. Ew. Pretty pitiful, huh? You know how, in magazines, columnists try to assuage lover's guilt over fantasizing someone other than their S.O.? Well, I sometimes fantasize that I'm someone else. That's a new one for me.

I know someone whom I'm madly drawn to, like a kamikaze, as if they were someone I'd known forever and trust implicitly (although, in fact, I have good reason to be wary), who would say I'm being self indulgent and that everyone feels that way. But thinking about stuff like this makes me lonely. Why?

Love, Erika H. in Portland

Dear Erika,

My, we are in a metaphysical funk, aren't we? It's fortunate you wrote to Uncle Mike promptly since any delay might have cured your angst before Uncle Mike had a chance to put in his two cents worth.

Is there anything that would make Uncle Mike want to stop living? Absolutely. Death, for one. Intractable physical pain is another. Or the belief he was of no use to anyone. Or forgetting the words to Me and Bobby McGee.

Is there anything or anyone Uncle Mike cannot live without? Certainly. After oxygen, water, and food come cigarettes, coffee, poker, and an occasional carafe of sour mash whiskey. Other humans? Although Uncle Mike has a great capacity for love and at least his fair allotment of friends, he has, like Bob Dylan, seen pretty people disappear like smoke. Over and over again. After a few such episodes, even chimpanzees get the picture. It's called nonattachment. Buddhists swear by it.

Why do you feel ineffectual? Misunderstanding. Since all actions have an effect, Uncle Mike can only assume you're in a profound state of inertia or are trapped inside your head. He suggests you do something besides listening raptly to the idiot monkey of your mind.

Why do you care? Probably because you're a caring person. Are you an egomaniac? With all due respect, Uncle Mike must snort with laughter. Egomaniacs assume their difficulties are the result of the refusal of others to worship them. Your difficulties seem the result of your reluctance to appreciate yourself. In Uncle Mike's experience, the best humans are those who are constantly baffled by anyone being remotely interested in them.

Are you headed for disaster? Who knows? But if Uncle Mike was a betting man, and he is, he'd bet not. Intelligence and empathy are strong talismans against making the sort of bonehead mistakes that feed one's life into the cosmic shredder. You seem possessed of both.

Are you headed for disappointment? Of course, dear. Who among us is not? As far as Uncle Mike can see, the trick is to have the fewest possible expectations and the greatest possible curiosity. Dreams, yes; hopes, absolutely; expectations, nope. To expect implies the ability to predict the future. Given life in a nondeterministic universe, it often leads to pain and sadness. Being in the world and not of it and working without lust for result are the prayers most often answered.

That you've lost your ability to dream seems, in Uncle Mike's experience, a short term disability, a symptom rather than a terminal disease. You haven't stopped dreaming, you've stopped remembering your dreams. This can mean a number of things, none of them more serious than a cognitive hangnail. Uncle Mike has had dream cycles he'd give a year of his life to get back. He suspects that's why they're gone.

That you've lost your ability to fantasize sexually is a slightly bigger deal. Uncle Mike sees it as either a need to get laid or an indication you're not feeling especially sexual just now. He'd wager his old mother's pension that the fantasies, and the realities, will return.

Uncle Mike is sad that you are sad. Even sadder that you're spiritually bereft. He senses the real problem is that you're feeling lonely and isolated and wounded by love. Welcome to the human comedy. Unlike the person to whom you're madly drawn, Uncle Mike doesn't think you're being self indulgent. Uncle Mike thinks you're being an introspective human, one of Uncle Mike's favorite kinds.

Most of all, Uncle Mike thinks you're hanging out with people who, for one reason or another, aren't your people. People who are your people exhibit certain behaviors. They appreciate you for who you are, they care about your well being and act in ways that support your sense of self, they accept the gift of your friendship with gratitude and respect and, most importantly, they give more than they take.

No, Erika, you're not unlovable. You're probably not even unloved. Uncle Mike suggests you find the nearest rose and smell it. Or run off with him for a wild weekend in Scappoose.

● ● ●

Dear Uncle Mike,

I learned recently that my fourteen year old daughter, we'll call her Monica, has stopped wearing panties. I don't count myself as a prude, but I must admit I'm concerned. She says she's not sexually active and for the most part I believe her. She says a lot of her friends don't wear underwear and that she feels more comfortable without it. What do you think?

Concerned Mom in Portland

Dear Mom,

About what?

Before Uncle Mike rolls up his sleeves to deal with your problem, he'd first like to point out you don't have one. On the off chance you've just emerged from a long coma, Mr. Rogers' neighborhood is not what it once was. Children your daughter's age carry guns, shoot drugs, mug pensioners, and set winos on fire. Having established perspective, Uncle Mike moves on.

If you're looking for moral support, you've knocked

on the wrong window. Although Uncle Mike wears underwear himself, he sees no reason for the rest of humanity to follow him like so many sheep. If Monica and her friends feel more comfortable with one less layer of fashion, more power to them. Albert Einstein gave up wearing socks and still turned out okay.

Uncle Mike wonders, what exactly is your concern? That your daughter is slightly more naked than you thought she was? Who in their right mind would have the time to care? As long as young Monica favors pants and knee length skirts, her choice shouldn't pose a threat, either to herself or polite society. What are you worrying, that she's turned into a teenage mutant slut? All things are certainly possible but, unless you've got more data than you've trotted out, Uncle Mike would caution against leaping to stupid conclusions.

To test his convictions, Uncle Mike spent a day without underwear. He didn't feel one bit more lascivious. He only felt cold.

● ● ●

Dear Uncle Mike,

My friend and I have a bet. I say since you're a whiny, self-righteous liberal, you voted yes on Measure 16, the so called Right to Die initiative. For once your opinion is worth twenty bucks to me.

Reluctant Reader in Garibaldi

Dear Repugnant Reader,

My, we certainly know how to put our best foot forward, don't we Muffin? Before telling that you how he voted is even less your business than the details of his mating habits, Uncle Mike would like to suggest a place to put your mush-brain stereotypes. While Uncle Mike may be, on occasion, whiny and self righteous, he would cheerfully open a vein before being a liberal. Uncle Mike is a full-blown leftist; which, in today's political climate, makes him a conservative democratic independent who sees George Bush and Rush Limbaugh as registered fascists. If you want the truth, Uncle Mike is also a little worried about Madonna.

As a conservative humanist, Uncle Mike devoutly believes that our bodies and all their contents, to include urine and fetuses, belong to the spirit inhabiting them. Who else, pray tell, would have ownership? In the words of Patrick Henry, Oliver North's hero: give us liberty or give us death. In some cases, they amount to the same thing.

● ● ●

Dear Uncle Mike,
My girlfriends and I have started an Uncle Mike fan club. We want to know if you're married, or have a girlfriend, and how old you are. Also if you're cute?
Julie and Friends, Eugene

Dear Julie et al,
While Uncle Mike is flattered beyond words that you and your addled friends have made him the object of your obsessions, he wonders if you might not want to change your drug dosage. Praying that, if he humors you, you

and your unbalanced little flock won't show up on his porch some night, Uncle Mike will answer your nosy questions.

Is Uncle Mike married? No. He was once, long ago. The decade-long episode proved to him that the lust for experience is stronger than the will to survive. Uncle Mike is now a well adjusted serial monogamist. He is not at the moment attached, unless you count the gentlemen in his poker support group.

How old is Uncle Mike? Depending on when you ask him, he's either younger than springtime or older than dirt. If Uncle Mike were a black lab, which he will be next time, he'd be a little more than 350 in human years.

Is Uncle Mike cute? You bet. Especially in the morning in his wrinkled bunny pajamas.

● ● ●

Dear Uncle Mike,

Last month you said if you were a black lab you'd be 350 in human years. I take that to mean you're fifty. I just turned fifty myself and I confess it's hit me in ways I hadn't expected. My health is good and all that (we won't talk about prostates, okay?) but I'm starting to think in terms of the old three score and ten and how that leaves me maybe twenty years. Twenty years ago seems like yesterday. Young women I'd flirt with if I weren't married are calling me "sir." Looking at myself in the bathroom mirror isn't as fun as it used to be. I realize that dreams I still nurture are probably not going to be. Nothing about my life has changed. I have a wonderful wife, grown children I love, and a job that's more fulfilling than most. Suddenly, it doesn't seem like enough. Is this a midlife crisis? Is there a cure?

                                        Feeling Old in Astoria

Dear Feeling Old,

Interesting word, crisis. What it means is a level of energy immediately preceding a change in the prevailing order. Given that nothing in the universe is more constant than change, Uncle Mike always counsels against resisting it. Midlife crisis is an unfortunate term coined by those overly mired in the inertia of youth and only a nitwit would look for a cure. Fiftieth birthdays should be celebrated with all the fervor of a puberty rite.

So young women are calling you "sir." What exactly do you have against respect? You are now, like it or not, a village elder. The deal we all make with space/time is to trade youth for experience. All things considered, Uncle Mike sees this as one of life's great bargains. Yes, Uncle Mike is 350 in dog years. Although he enjoyed a charmed and amusing youth, his portion of the human comedy didn't even start getting fun until he hit forty. Life, like poker, is more fun when you understand the rules.

No, Uncle Mike is not thrilled with his stomach tone. This only means the scant seconds he once spent in front of the mirror admiring his never especially exciting physique can be turned to more productive use trimming his ear hair. Try as he might, Uncle Mike can't muster any pain and sadness from growing older.

He is, in fact, happy as a clam to have lived half a century and would open a vein before going back even to yesterday.

As for dreams, Uncle Mike regards himself as the laughable result of his. No, they haven't all worked out as he planned. On his way to Oz, he wound up in a metaphorical cabin in the coast range and giggles a lot at his luck. In a spherical universe whose center is everywhere, all paths lead to home. The only dream Uncle Mike still thinks worth dreaming is to be at peace with his world. At any age, the only

game in town is understanding: knowing our place in the cosmic minuet and dancing the best we can. Uncle Mike is reconciled to the fact he'll never be James Dean. These days, he'd rather be Robert Duvall.

Having feelings of mortality, are we? Good for you. Uncle Mike can only wonder where you've been. Feeling gloomy? Uncle Mike wonders where you are. Yes, by standards set by the American Medical Society, we're all going to croak. Men our age drop over like pole-axed steers every day of the week and Uncle Mike bets not one of them saw it coming. It could happen, heaven forbid, before you finish reading this. At the risk of sounding callous, Uncle Mike must ask, so what? As Wendell Berry pointed out in his novel, "Memory of Old Jack" (for which he should have won the Nobel Prizes for both Peace and Literature): it is no tragedy when, at the end of a life, a man dies.

The handmaiden of age is, or at least should be, wisdom. A good part of wisdom, perhaps all of it, is knowing who and where we are. Forget that pewling homily, "This is the first day of the rest of your life." It could jolly well be our last day on the planet and only a nitwit would fail to act accordingly. That nitwit is youth.

Uncle Mike does, however, welcome the opportunity not to speak of prostates.

● ● ●

Dear Uncle Mike,

I've got this problem. Actually, my boyfriend does. This woman at his office is hustling him. She works under him, no pun intended, and her behavior is obvious to everyone. My boyfriend has consistently turned down invitations to lunch and drinks after work. He says he's made his lack of interest clear but the woman just won't take a hint. She's an excellent worker and he doesn't want to let her go, but the situation is getting on both our nerves. Any suggestions?

Pissed Off in Portland

Dear Pissed Off,

First off, congratulations on believing your boyfriend when he says the flirtation is a one-way affair. A lesser woman might call him a lying dog and demand he fire her or find a new place for his toothbrush.

Uncle Mike suggests your boyfriend draft an office memo dealing with the federal statutes on sexual harassment in the workplace. If anyone's amorous pursuits, male or female, interferes with the object of their affection's ability to function on the job, it constitutes indictable crime.

If this doesn't cool her jets, Uncle Mike suggests you give the little hussy a call. Ask if she has any pictures showing what she looked like with all her front teeth. Explain that you see her behavior as a personal assault on your pursuit of happiness and any further batting of the eyes could lead to a nasty introduction to your Rottweiler.

●●●

Dear Uncle Mike,

How do I endure loneliness? How do I deal with that restless feeling in my gut that makes me face the reality that I'm not enjoying my life. I scare myself contemplating the solutions to this problem.

I've always thought that with friends you can get through pretty much anything. There is one person who really cares about me, and I grew up with him. He's away at college. I love him more than anything. I'm happy when I'm with him.

So my question is this: How am I to overcome this painful isolation. Believe me I've tried. Is life even worth it without friends: I'm definitely looking forward to college.

Lynn in Seaside

Dear Lynn,

Is life worth living without friends? Probably not. Fortunately, you have one. Sadly, you're separated from him. This makes you, for the moment, alone. Alone is a neutral state. Being lonely is your decision, and it's a stupid and nasty one.

People will tell you loneliness is part of life. They'll be either fools or liars. Loneliness is not the inevitable, or even a natural, result of being alone. What it is, is an inappropriate response to temporal reality. The hollowness you feel comes from deciding not to accept what is.

No dear, Uncle Mike isn't denying the state of Siamese twinship that love triggers in all of us; that joining at the heart and the gut which, when severed, makes two complete humans feel half of who they were. Uncle Mike has, Lord knows, been there. But he's learned that missing someone is one thing and obsessing on the void they've left is quite another. Loneliness is the mistaking of want for need, the illusion of the half empty cup, the idiot notion that the tides of the universe have gone out and will never return.

Being all but human, Uncle Mike is no stranger to this sort of gloomy nitwittery and doesn't for a moment underestimate its ability to paralyze will power, good cheer, and the ability to perform simple acts of reason. Yes, he's wallowed more times than he cares to remember and has the bad poetry to prove it. He finally realized this: lovers have a delightful knack for living inside each other. No matter where you are, there they are. People have been known to write good poems about this. You should give it a shot.

How to overcome the pain of isolation? The only thing that alters inertia, a polite term for the dead weight you life seems to have become, is change in motion. Get out of the house, woman, and into whoever you are. Whatever you enjoy doing, do it, often and completely. Uncle Mike doubts you have only one friend. Seek out the company of others. Silly as it sounds, you should have some fun. Tried all this, have we? Good. Try it again. The trick to magic is to not stop doing it until it works.

Uncle Mike is glad you're looking forward to college. Aside from brutal experience, education is the shortest path to understanding.

● ● ●

Dear Uncle Mike,
    I have a large aquarium and am thinking of getting an octopus. Am I being foolish?
                                    Art S., Portland

Dear Art,

No, you're being a lunatic. Listen very carefully, Art. No matter how large your aquarium is, it's not large enough. Octopi may be mollusks but they're not stupid. Squished under it's rock, its disgusting tentacles curled coyly under its impossibly ugly face, your octopus will only seem to be whiling away the hours. It will be brooding, dreaming murderous dreams, and waiting for the moment you forget to wrap the tank with concertina wire. As your slimy nightmare drags you, shrieking and flailing, into its lair, you'll wish you'd stuck to goldfish.

● ● ●

Dear Uncle Mike,

I live in a small town. Last week, a friend told me she'd been hearing rumors. Without getting into them, they're totally unfounded and completely out of character for me. I haven't lived here long enough for everyone to know better. Should I confront the situation or ignore it?

Innocent in Astoria

Dear Reasonably Innocent,

Uncle Mike would suggest a combination of both. Unless those spreading the rumors are much larger than you or are known to carry weapons, wait for a public opportunity to help them put their ducks in a row. Within earshot of at least two other people, tell them their mouth seems much larger than their brain and that, in addition to having the ethics of a rabid weasel, they're full of crap and should dummy up and get a life. Uncle Mike assumes the people in your life who really count know what's up with you. The opinions of others deserve to be roundly ignored. The banishing ritual for false rumor is to live the truth.

● ● ●

Dear Uncle Mike,

This is kind of a weird question, but you write a weird column so I thought I'd give it a shot. My problem is my girlfriend. She thinks she's fat. Not only is she not fat, she's not even overweight. In fact, she's got a great body. For a while, I thought she wasn't serious, that she was just fishing for compliments or something. It's got to the point she doesn't even want me to see her naked. I'm really serious about her but it's starting to be a problem. Any suggestions?

Tony R., Eugene

Dear Tony,

Uncle Mike has many suggestions. The first is to not ask advice from those you first insult. Uncle Mike writes a weird column, does he? At least he doesn't punish himself by hanging with neurotic females obsessed with their weight. No, that's a lie. Being male, heterosexual, and unwilling to become a monk, Uncle Mike has learned that dealing with women who think they're fat is part of the gig. It's a great life if you don't buckle.

First off, Fluffy, let's be sure we're dealing with reality. Is the woman mildly porkish, or not? Granted, she's beautiful to you, but if she could stand to cut back on the Alfredo and bonbons, denying things won't make it less true. No, you should not tell her this. Trust Uncle Mike, nothing lies in that direction but pain, regret, and the very real chance of physical attack. You should merely support her in her attempt to reach what is almost certainly the unattainable.

Know this: in a poll taken by professionals who busy themselves asking strangers what they think, something like eighty percent of American women are dissatisfied with what they see in the mirror. Large industries have been built on perpetuating this hate affair our sisters have with themselves. Uncle Mike believes the problem could be largely solved if women spent less time looking into mirrors, a method with which he's had great personal success. He's yet to find a woman willing to embrace the discipline.

You ask if your friend's obsession with body tissue is neurotic? You bet. So is the male's usual obsession with mammary glands and gluteal muscle. Two ends of the same stick. Her compulsion to meet standards set by those who want to sell her cosmetics, exercise machines, and liquid diets is no accident. It's a crime not just against gender but against all of humanity and it'll stop when we all quit buying into it.

Uncle Mike's advice to you is this: at every opportunity, praise your woman to the heavens. One of the few healthy attitudes about gender Norman Mailer ever expressed was that most of the problems between men and women would go away if, at least once a day, men told women they were beautiful and women told men they were brave.

●●●

Dear Uncle Mike,
  Do you think O.J. is guilty? I do.

                    Convinced in Portland

Dear Convinced,

  Like you, Uncle Mike hasn't the foggiest notion. Unlike you, he reserves his opinion for things he knows something about.

  Guilty or innocent (legal terms, by the way), can you imagine how much fun it must have been for Mr. Simpson (Uncle Mike doesn't know the man and cannot call him O.J.) to have millions of half-baked, bloodthirsty nitwits willing to hang you before the jury hears all the evidence? Isn't it great to live in a country where it's okay to have opinions without benefit of facts and rational thought?

  Uncle Mike knows two things about the O.J. Simpson trial. The first is that, while Russians are slaughtering Chechens, Serbs are massacring Muslims, and Mexicans are strafing Mayans, his fellow Americans are watching Kato Kaelin and obsessing about a glove. The second thing Uncle Mike knows is that it makes him want to vomit.

● ● ●

Dear Uncle Mike,
  Where do you stand on spanking children?

                    Darryl P., Portland

Dear Darryl,

Uncle Mike regards spanking as an act best restricted to consenting adults. He finds this acceptable, if odd. As a means of improving the behavior of children, he finds it laughable and sadistic. By the time that violence delivered upon someone smaller and more innocent than you seems appropriate, the adult involved is in a state far too irrational to administer judgment. The first rule of civilization is that nobody hits.

● ● ●

Dear Uncle Mike,

The other night, my husband and I went out for dinner. Nothing fancy, just a nice place. The couple two tables over brought their five year old and we spent the whole meal listening to the child whining and her parents cajoling and threatening her. I was furious. My husband says I should have let it ruin my meal, that kids will be kids. I say the management should have done something. What do you think?

Furious in Eugene

Dear Furious,

Uncle Mike thinks the world is going to hell in a hand-basket and that your night out does nothing to lessen his suspicions.

When Uncle Mike was a child, his parents took him to pizza parlors and Chinese restaurants. Although it might have occurred to him to behave badly, he didn't; not because he was a young saint, but because he'd been taught through lessons mild and harsh to mind his manners. By today's standards, or lack of them, Uncle Mike would be thought horribly repressed.

Uncle Mike was further stunted by media images of children who showed respect for their parents. He did not imagine that the world revolved around him or that adults were stupid and oppressive louts given to him to shape up. Then again, Uncle Mike was blessed to grow up in a time when adults were easier to respect.

This brings us to your dinner. To Uncle Mike's way of thinking, this issue isn't restaurant management. The issue is parenting and the lack thereof. Which brings us to Uncle Mike's rules for dining out with your child. The first whine is free. The second whine gets a bone-chilling warning. The third whine and the kid's out of there. No alibis, no excuses, no plea bargains. Big dogs rolling over for puppies is a violation of the natural order.

Should you have let the little whelp's floor show ruin your meal? Short of asking your server for earplugs or changing your order to takeout, Uncle Mike sees no way it couldn't have. Should the management have done something? If they didn't expect the occasional childish outburst, they'd draw a line five feet up the wall and post a sign saying, 'If you're not this big, you shouldn't be here'.

The question you didn't ask was, should I have done something? Not to be nasty but Uncle Mike feels this makes you part of the problem. Next time, fix the little family with a cold-eyed stare. If this fails of result, approach the table and as if there's anything you could possibly do to make their domestic tableau less dysfunctional. They'll get huffy and tell you to mind your own business. Tell them politely that you are.

Remind them that it takes a whole village to raise a child and, if they'd like, you'll be happy to shove a large cork into the mouth of theirs.

Dear Uncle Mike,
 Do you think marijuana should be legal?
 Sheila W., Eugene

Dear Sheila,
 In a word, yes. Uncle Mike believes all drugs should be both legal and dirt cheap, and that the tax from their regulated sales would help finance the sort of society in which twelve-year-olds with Uzis don't sell crack on bicycles. Uncle Mike believes the most dangerous drug is money. After that comes gasoline.
 If we're speaking in terms of social disease, drug abuse (and here Uncle Mike thinks mostly of alcohol, cocaine, heroin, Valium, and Prozac) is most correctly seen as a symptom. Genetic disposition aside, humans with reason to hope don't smoke crack, shoot black tar, or drink themselves into a stupor on a regular basis. Humans who "abuse" drugs are medicating themselves against a toxic reality. With seventy percent of federal prison inmates incarcerated for drug-related crime, Uncle Mike wonders if the war on drugs might be better waged on poverty, injustice, and despair.
 Uncle Mike also wonders if marijuana can be called a dangerous drug. Cannabis may sap smokers of the energy and drive necessary to trade stock or set sales records but, as many have pointed out, potheads don't knock over convenience stores for the price of a joint. Potheads giggle and eat Milk Duds. Unlike the beer and martini afflicted, potheads can touch their noses with their fingers (often doing it for a lark) and nearly never drive their cars into solid objects at high speeds.
 Is marijuana a social problem? Uncle Mike must snort. In his experience, smokers of hemp are more interesting than drunks, more dependable than coke freaks,

less likely to steal your stereo than heroin addicts, and much more fun than the Prozacked. As for being good citizens, marijuana devotees are, if anything, too considerate and thoughtful, displaying an appreciation for the subtle wonders of the here and now that borders on the religious. This is a quality Uncle Mike enjoys in his fellow humans.

● ● ●

Dear Uncle Mike,

Do you know anything about birds? I want to get one but I don't know what kind. My mom reads your column and thinks you're pretty smart. She said to ask you. I'm eight. Thank you.

Julie T., Portland

Dear Julie,

Uncle Mike is glad you wrote. Because he's Uncle Mike, he'd hate to see you make the mistake of your life before you reach teenagerdom.

Does Uncle Mike know anything about birds? Only enough to keep him from sharing his home with them. What kind of bird should you get? Uncle Mike recommends a stuffed one. It might be boring but at least you'll be able to sleep without a scattergun. Listen carefully, Julie. Beneath the chirping and the bright feathers and fluff, birds are winged reptiles directly descended from dinosaurs. Did you see "Jurassic Park," Julie? To birds, those were the good old days.

Don't let canaries and parakeets fool you, kid. They don't seem like much but, in their bloodthirsty little dreams, they stand forty feet at the shoulder and see you as part of the food chain. When push comes to shove, and one day it will, you'll learn your little Tweetie has all the compassion of a cobra.

Single canaries are okay as long as the cage is welded steel. Never,
never get a pair. The smaller species are twisted little sociopaths who tend to egg each other on. Trust Uncle Mike, sweetie. If lovebirds were granted their deepest wishes, no one would call them lovebirds.

If you're flat out determined to live with a bird, Uncle Mike thinks you should go for the real deal and get a large raptor. Something like a buzzard. Or perhaps a barn owl. Raptors are what your budgie would be if it had access to steroids: a vicious, winged predator who would kill before bursting into song. If you're looking for looking for truth, nothing compares to watching your vulture launch itself from the mantel in another try for the cat.

• • •

Dear Uncle Mike,
My husband and I have been married for five years. I don't think he's ever been faithful. He's made "stupid mistakes" three times with "women who mean nothing" to him. I suspect there've been other flings I don't know about. I knew he was a womanizer when I married him but I thought he'd change. I'm writing because I think he's fooling around again. I don't want to leave him, in a lot of ways he's the right man for me, but I can't take this much longer. What do I say to him? What do I do? Any suggestions would be most appreciated.
Sleepless in Tigard

Letters to Uncle Mike

Dear Witless,

Uncle Mike's first suggestion is to get your head examined. You're married to a philandering weasel who doesn't give a rat's rump for your feelings. Ditch the bum. Quit with the rationalizations. Who cares if he means well? Who cares if he suffers from a Peter Pan syndrome? Who cares what wounded him as a child and arrested his emotional development? Who cares if his ego needs extra gratification as part of the healing process? Aside from Oprah, no one. We are what we do and what he's doing stinks.

Uncle Mike would love to share with you some mantra which, were your husband to recite it daily, would help him keep his trousers on. Uncle Mike would love to say that if you just hang in there things will change. Uncle Mike must instead suggest that you wake up and smell the garbage. You can't trust the man. Without trust, there is no marriage. Without trust, there isn't even friendship.

If one has affairs (Uncle Mike is not entirely divorced from a real world in which forty percent of the women and sixty percent of the men say they have), one at least owes discretion and restraint. Your husband shows neither. Violating vows of fidelity is one thing, rubbing your mate's nose in it is another. Your husband is either a hopeless emotional bungler or he just doesn't care. Uncle Mike suspects both.

All of which boils down to this. He's who he is, you're who you are, and life, as they say, is short. Unless you're willing to live out the status quo for the rest of your piece of forever, tell the bum one more time that you're serious. Have him repeat the words, never again. When next he trips over his libido, and Uncle Mike would bet his granny's pension he will, cut your losses and carve him out of your life like the wart he is.

Dear Uncle Mike,
What do you think happens when you die?
Erin R., Portland

Dear Erin,

Not much, if you listen to some people. Uncle Mike doesn't. Uncle Mike is a closet quantum physicist and, having seen no evidence of death in the physical universe, sees no reason to buy into the notion of grim reapers. Uncle Mike is not being a nitwit. He knows full well that, one sunny day, he's going to drop in his tracks like a pole-axed steer. Uncle Mike doesn't see this as death. He sees it as recycling.

Here's the deal, Erin. When pondering the great beyond and our place in it, the first thing you want to remember is the conservation of mass/energy. In a universe that's both closed and unbounded, nothing is lost, nothing is gained. Physical systems, our bodies among them, deteriorate and lose integrity, their little quantum components cease to work in concert and go their separate ways. Uncle Mike fails to see the tragedy.

So much for the physical world. The real question is, when we say "I" what do we mean? Is there something about us that isn't our physical body? Something that's in the world but not of it. Of the many ways to pursue this question, Uncle Mike's favorite is Von Neumann's Chain.

John Von Neumann was a quantum physicist of the first rank who invented the logic of the stored program computer, which is to say the computer as we know it. He also pioneered in cybernetics, discovered game theory, and wrote a text that's referred to as "the quantum Bible." One day he set out to answer the simplest of questions: why is there anything?

Von Neumann began with the basics. Quantum

theory, the most successful idea in the history of science, rests on the quantum effect. Simply put, the physical world manifests itself in discrete bits: the quanta. The proton, electron, neutron, photon, and neutrino combine to form all that is and their interactions are the forces of nature. Most simply put, the universe arises from difference. Von Neumann's question was, where does difference arise? Why is there a universe at all?

This is no longer a metaphysical issue. The equations of quantum physics make it very clear that the universe of our perceptions is a thin foam of object/events on the surface of an apparently infinite sea of unmanifest probabilities. At any point in space/time, a vast array of possible realities exist, some of them more likely than others. In order for there to be anything, all possible somethings but the one we observe must somehow disappear, the likelihood of their occurrence reduced to zero my some statistical deus ex machina: the god, or the ghost, in the machine. Quantum physics calls this event, the birth of the universe on a point scale, "the collapse of probabilities."

Von Neumann's question thus becomes, what triggers the collapse of what might be into what is? What is it that makes something of nothing?

To find out, Von Neumann constructed a logical schematic of quantum reality now called "Von Neumann's Chain." The chain consists of three links: a source, a signal, and a receiver. Von Neumann could imagine no simpler system since, if any of these elements are removed, nothing in the way of observable (quantum) reality can occur. The trouble is, there's nothing unique about the links. At bottom, they're made of same unmanifest prob-abilities ("quantum stuff") as everything else.

At the level of "deep reality," the universe that rests behind this one like a final Burma Shave sign saying nothing, source, signal, and receiver are one. Or, in theological terms, One.

Bear with Uncle Mike, Erin. There's really a point to all this.

Try as he might, and he's a very smart guy who tried very hard, Von Neumann could find no preferred, or even possible, site on the chain of quantum reality for the collapse of probabilities to take place. With the source? Just probabilities. The signal? More of the same. With the receiver (observer)? Not even there. The observer is no more holy or privileged than the source and signal of what it observes and none of them exist as discrete object/events. There is no place in quantum reality for difference (the quanta) to arise; and without difference, the distinction between one something and another, nothing can be shown to exist but the unbroken sameness of 'no thing'.

What Von Neumann was forced to conclude from this is pretty heady stuff. Whatever it is that collapses unmanifest potential into observable reality is not and cannot be part of that reality. Not just observed reality, but observable reality. Whatever transforms what might be into what is, it isn't part of what is. When Von Neumann, the man generally credited with framing quantum logic, asked himself what, if anything, lies outside the quantum universe, he could think of just one thing: consciousness. If quantum theory is an accurate picture of what is, its reason for being is the unseen wind that fills the sails of awareness. The universe is not a great machine, it's a great thought.

Okay, Erin, we're nearly home.

So if we go along with Von Neumann's Proof (and sixty years of searching hasn't produced a path around its logic), the universe arises from consciousness. Given this, it stands to reason that, for the universe to exist fully as the four- dimensional sphere Einstein thought it to be, its probabilities must be collapsed into quantum reality at every point in space/time. For an individual object/event to exist, it must be imbedded in an unbroken continuum of awareness; for the universe to exist, it must be, at all points, conscious.

So anyway, you were asking about death. By this, Uncle Mike assumes you mean the disappearance of the object of the personal pronoun "I." You can see how, in light of Von Neumann's Proof, dying becomes a little tricky. In a conscious universe, I-ness becomes point-conscious perspective: a unique vantage point in a seamless and endless act of creation. If any of these perspectives (the one called Erin, for instance) disappeared (where to, God only knows), some portion of the geometry of space/time would cease to exist. Since the universe exists, we must assume this has never happened.

Your question, yes, Uncle Mike remembers it, was: what happens when we die? The same thing that happens when we live. We keep noticing things we hadn't seen, go right on being point-conscious perspectives at play in the fields of space/time. No disrespect to priests and undertakers, but there's no room for death in the equations.

● ● ●

Dear Uncle Mike,

A good friend just inherited close to two million dollars. He's just an average guy in his forties, has a job and a life he likes. I love the guy like a brother but he has zero business sense. He plans to just put the money in the bank. I hooked him up with a stockbroker I know, but my friend seems unable to make a decision about what to do with his money. He reads you column and maybe if you said something he'd listen. I hate to see him miss out on building a nest egg for retirement. Can you help?

Vince R., Eugene

Dear Vince,

Uncle Mike would love to help. He's that sort of person. He does, however, shy away from fixing things that aren't broken. So your friend fell into a couple mil. Good for him. So he likes his job and his life. Gangbusters. Uncle Mike loves to hear happy stories and is sad to hear this one causes you distress. As his granny used to tell him, for every silver lining there's a cloud.

Uncle Mike has never found it in his heart to believe money is the root of all evil. Money is the root of many possibilities, one of which is to not let its presence or absence warp your perspective. Like any dangerous drug, it can become an end rather than a means. Very bad juju. Someone once asked J. Paul Getty how he managed to become the richest human on the planet, he answered that money had always been the most important thing in his life. To Uncle Mike, this makes him a junkie. When another someone mailed him his grandson's ear along with a request for an amount of cash J. Paul could have blown on lunch, the old jackal didn't budge.
Uncle Mike sees this as false grit.

So your friend is resisting the entreaties of a stockbroker. Uncle Mike likes him more by the minute. Yes, there are socially responsible investments: ventures that don't involve some sort of rape and pillage (hundred dollar sneakers, third world sweatshops, toxic moneyfills). And yes, there are socially conscious stockbrokers, poltergeists in the machinery of the leveraged buyout. Sadly, they make their daily croissants on commissions.

111

As sharks must swim to breathe, brokers must buy and sell. To say a broker will encourage you to keep turning your money like compost is to understate the case. Maybe your friend doesn't want to be bothered thinking about the care and feeding of money.

And, by Uncle Mike's figures, he hardly needs to. So the hopeless idiot wants to just sock his two million away in a bank. Even passbook interest on it would be (put down the zero, carry the one)...Holy Moly! Ninety thousand bucks a year. Unless his retirement plans include marrying Imelda Marcos, this should keep him in shoes.

Your friend seems to have mastered one of life's great challenges: being content with what you have. You, on the other hand, seem to wrestling unsuccessfully with another: learning to mind your own business. Uncle Mike wishes you both long life and prosperity.

● ● ●

Dear Uncle Mike,

I'm 32, attractive, intelligent, and single. I think I love you. Are you married? Are you cute? Do you ever date your fans?

Alicia M., Portland

Dear Alicia,

Forget to take our medicine, did we dear? Listen very carefully. You don't know Uncle Mike. It follows that you cannot be both intelligent and in love with him. Uncle Mike is flattered you find his disembodied projection worthy of daydreams. For Uncle Mike, it's Sinead

O'Connor and Lena Olin.

But, while Uncle Mike can obsess with the best of them, he'd open a vein before humiliating himself by writing to them.

Is Uncle Mike married? Only to his bad habits, his personality defects, and to a devout reluctance to inflict them on someone he loves.

Is Uncle Mike cute? Kittens, puppies, and greeting cards are cute. On a good day, Uncle Mike looks like the old dog he is. Except for the straw hat.

Does Uncle Mike ever date his fans? Uncle Mike doesn't date. He tried it as a youth and wound up horribly confused, and neither his nurse nor his poker support group feel it's time yet. Uncle Mike hangs with friends. Sometimes they sleep over and we buy each other breakfast.

● ● ●

Dear Uncle Mike,

I read in the papers Elaine Franklin, Senator Packwood's right hand woman, makes $136,000 a year. Can this be right?

Jeff S., Salem

Dear Jeff,

Interesting word, "right." If you define it in the context of childcare workers making five dollars an hour and single parent waitresses being taxed on their tips, then no. If your question is really, how much would it take to persuade a normal human being to shill for a lecherous scumbag with the political ethics of a diseased weasel, $136,000 isn't a whole lot of money.

Having met Elaine Franklin, Uncle Mike honestly believes she's worth every penny. He only wishes neither of them were allowed to play with the other children.

• • •

Dear Uncle Mike,

Perhaps your readers, who seem to mistake you for a lantern of rationality, would be interested in hearing why you don't eat shrimp or crab. You're as neurotic and dysfunctional as the rest of us, you big phony.

A Friend, Cannon Beach

Dear Acquaintance,

Uncle Mike has never denied being neurotic and dysfunctional. Anyone who can be paralyzed by the sight of mayonnaise can lay few claims on normalcy. He can certainly relate to your scorn. It shocks him as much as you that people, many of them adults, not only ask his advice but listen without laughing. To think they might act on it only makes Uncle Mike more wary when moving among them. Still, as grandma said when we loaded her into the van, life's what it is and a person's got to make the best of it.

Since, for reasons Uncle Mike is happy not to know, you confuse his affairs for your own, you're probably aware his avoidance of shell fish (ha, there's a joke) is a recently acquired distaste. For most of his life, a life riddled with questionable habits, Uncle Mike ate crab and shrimp, at times with abandon. He stopped eating them ten years ago, along with lobster and crayfish, the moment he realized what they are.

'Shell fish', for anyone with eyes to see and the brains God gave a shell fish, are underwater insects. In a word, bugs. Aberrant behavior can be fun, heaven knows, but Uncle Mike draws the line at eating bugs. In terms of what Uncle Mike would eat out of desperation, large underwater insects come several clicks after bark. Call it silly, but a man must stand for something. Uncle Mike stands for never putting anything that ugly into your mouth.

● ● ●

Dear Uncle Mike,

My question today is this: why don't children these days say 'thank you'? For a while I thought my irritation with this was mostly my over-developed need for appreciation, but as time goes by, I am becoming more discouraged daily.

There are many children in my life, my own, my nieces, nephews, and friends, etc. In the past several years I've only received two written thank you's from a young person after hosting them at my house or giving a gift. Rarely do I hear, "Can I help with dinner?" or "Thanks for the great meal." I don't think I've ever heard, "Now what can I do for you?"

This is turning me into a Scrooge. Whose problem are we talking about, mine or the kids'?

Unappreciated on the North Coast

115

Dear Unappreciated,

Perhaps the greatest political wisdom is that we get the government we deserve. The same can be said for children. It takes a whole village to raise a rude and thoughtless child.

What's to be done about it? A revival of good parenting pops to mind. Like you, Uncle Mike was taught to say please, thank you, and excuse me. Like you, he learned that work is shared and help is always offered. Like you, he was encouraged to think of others at least part of the time. Like you, Uncle Mike often feels like a dinosaur.

Somewhere between Dr. Spock, primal therapy, and EST, the American village, and most of the parents in it, embraced the nitwit notion that teaching manners to children is a subtle form of social oppression that stunts their will to be. Or not be, or whatever. Uncle Mike feels what manners stunt is the child's will to be a pint sized barbarian. Without what used to be called social graces, there is no civilization. There is only a life-style, and a boorish one at that.

Because parents are busy sort of fulfillment only time saving devices and the home shopping network can bring, they scarcely have the energy to say please and thank you themselves. The village has, by default, subcontracted the socialization of apprentice humans to television. History will view this as a nasty mistake. There are no manners on popular television, there are only motives.

You ask whose problem this is. Uncle Mike would suppose anyone who notices there's a problem. Certainly, parents are intimately responsible for the social behavior of their children. Imitation is the most sincere form of childhood and one of the most charming, and frightening, things about children is the way they mirror their environment, all of it. The adults of the village must, one by one, accept that being an adult implies a responsibility to all children.

Part of that responsibility lies in teaching the little whelps some manners. In his dealings with children, Uncle Mike gives respect and courtesy and insists it be returned. When it's not, he assumes his role as village elder and delivers a gentle but firm teaching called, Little Dog, Big Dog. Unless, of course, the child is over eleven and could be packing a gun.

●●●

Dear Uncle Mike,

As one man to another, do you ever think a significant part of premenstrual syndrome is self-indulgence? Are women as out of control as they'd like us to believe, or they just taking their suffering out on us? Should they be indulged? At what cost?

Victimized in Portland

Dear Victimized,

Because Uncle Mike doesn't believe in death and so doesn't fear it, he'll resist the urge to pretend your letter never reached him. As one man to another, Uncle Mike would suggest you stop asking questions like this. Premenstrual women can detect innuendo at great distance.

Does Uncle Mike think PMS is partly self-indulgent? No. Uncle Mike thinks it's altogether self-indulgent. It's from this its great horror springs. The lunar chemical imbalance women go through, many would say entirely

117

too often, evidently makes the world, and every unsatisfactory and irritating bit of it, a personal matter. The way you daub your mouth with a napkin can be, for she who yells, a snide reference to imaginary weight gain. The formulas of body chemistry are no laughing matter, and this one seems to prevent so much as a thought of self-restraint. The blurting out of lunatic venom and accusation can be, from safe distance, a sight to behold.

You ask if our ladies of the moon are as out of control as they'd like us to believe. Man to man, Uncle Mike dares you to find out. He only hopes they're as out of control as they'll get. As it is, he's seen them do things that curled his hair and made him sleep lightly. Are they taking their suffering out on us? Is this a serious question? Uncle Mike has seen the chemically unbalanced take it out on furniture, small animals, and trees. Any portion of the world will do, but the universal law governing the chaos of their emotions seems to dictate that, the closer they feel to you, the more efficient the abuse gets. Should we indulge them? If you've got a better idea, Uncle Mike is all ears. Until then, he'll go on indulging them whenever it's not possible to avoid their company. He avoids them with great zeal and sees this as giving them their space.

Uncle Mike read a story once about a primitive tribe whose women would, in response to mysterious inner signals, walk a short distance from the village and build a small getaway hut. Uncle Mike sees this as genius, and wonders that any culture but theirs has survived.

●●●

Dear Uncle Mike,
　　Why are potatoes called 'spuds'?
　　　　　　　　　　　　Robert D., Molalla

Dear Robert,
　　Before he begins, Uncle Mike would like to thank you for your question. Other people ask Uncle Mike advice on personal matters the details of which he'd rather not know. You ask about potatoes. Uncle Mike likes you.
　　Potatoes are called spuds not because they were invented by someone with a silly sounding name, but because of a confusion. A spud is a tool, a tree branch cleverly carved by hungry rustics. It has a long handle and a foot piece which, when pressed down by the foot, makes a six inch deep hole in the dirt. The potato is, of course, what you put in the hole. It's a funny world.

● ● ●

Dear Uncle Mike,
　　Where do you stand on the issue of killing the rude?
　　　　　　　　　　Your bartender, Cannon Beach

Dear Holiness,
　　Uncle Mike likes your question nearly as much as the one about spuds. Uncle Mike is, darn, pretty much opposed to killing anybody. Not because he's nice, but because it doesn't really change things. Like large caricatures of children, the rude must be taught to behave. As a member of the service, or servant, sector of the

American dream, you're given many opportunities to deliver the teaching.

Within the guidelines set by the person able to fire you, never let the rude confuse you with personal staff. Explain, with as much charm as you can muster that you're here to provide a service, not to be the service provided. As a human, you're not part of the bill and any dealings you have with each other must be based on at least the appearance of mutual respect. Without civilized behavior on their part, all bets are off. Assure them they don't want to see that.

Uncle Mike heard a nice story about a waitress who'd reached critical mass. Leaning over the offending couple's table, she said in menacing, maternal tones, "Listen, if we play together any longer, we're going to quarrel. I work here, so it's you who gets to leave." A statue should be built to this woman.

●●●

Dear Uncle Mike,

I just moved into my boyfriend's house and already we've got problems. I'm not Miss Popularity or anything, but I've got a lot of friends and they like to stop by. They don't always call first and this drives him crazy. He's more reclusive than me and he says he feels like he has no privacy, that he never knows who's going to knock on the door. I feel like I'm being separated from my friends who I think should be able to visit whenever they want to. Am I being unreasonable or is he?

Feeling Isolated in Beaverton

Dear Isolated,

First off, let Uncle Mike say that living in Beaverton is, by itself, enough to make the normal feel isolated. If the friends you're talking about live there by choice, you may be better off alone. This said, we press on. Uncle Mike doesn't see your little piece of the human comedy as an either/or proposition. You're both behaving as if you lived alone, which may be an arrangement you should, as a couple, re-explore.

Let's begin by attacking you. Uncle Mike shares your boyfriend's feelings for people who 'drop by'. Right after gravity and the velocity of light, the first rule in Uncle Mike's universe is that we all call first. This is partly explained by Uncle Mike's being a devout hermit and partly by his having manners. On those rare occasions he thinks it would be nice to see old so and so, it would never occur to him that his restless urge to visit was synchronized with his victim's unspoken urge to entertain.

Unlike you, Uncle Mike doesn't have lots of friends. Uncle Mike has very few friends. He does have lots of acquaintances, many of them warm ones and is, as a rule, delighted when they call and leave a message on his machine. If Uncle Mike loves them a great deal, or they owe him money, and if he feels like dealing with another human being for any reason short of preserving life, he picks up the phone. If he doesn't, he assumes they'll assume he's not, as the houseboy would say, 'at home'. Not even Uncle Mike's blood relations drop by unannounced. They stopped when he began greeting unexpected visitors in the nude, a practice Uncle Mike has found wonderfully effective in winnowing lightweights from his social network. If you and he moved in together, only one of you would come out in the spring.

Now on to your jerk boyfriend. Uncle Mike can only

assume he knew your friends were a pack of mannerless louts before you began your little misadventure in cohabitation. This can only mean he expected the pleasure of his company would be enough for you, and that your domestic union would trigger a magical change in your social habits. On Uncle Mike's block, this makes him a drooling nitwit. Another of Uncle Mike's many first rules is that everyone gets to be who they are. Explain to him in very small words that, if living with him means giving up the rest of your human contacts, you'd be happy to call him from your new place before you drop by.

Make no mistake. Uncle Mike has great respect for the sacred institution of living together. He hopes with all his heart that, before the two of you bail on a situation from which you're both going to learn so much, you sit down together and look up 'compromise' in your Funk & Wagnall's. Uncle Mike did and was forced to reject the notion. He has since spent many happy years single-habiting out of love for the hapless women who, from time to time, wander through his life with lanterns, looking for just one man who measures up.

● ● ●

Dear Uncle Mike,
Do you think computers are going to take over the world?

Don C., Portland

Dear Don,

No, Uncle Mike thinks it's much worse than that. The world will be taken over by computer generated humans who imagine that virtual reality is the same as being there, that life can be programmed, and that the human experience is something that can be downloaded late. This is the error called, mistaking the tool for the work. In a history peppered with bouts of fuzzy thinking, this one promises to be a real pip.

●●●

Dear Uncle Mike,

I'm thirteen. My father won't let me listen to rap music. Do you think this is fair?

Anonymous, Cannon Beach

Dear Anonymous,

Of course not. But then, it doesn't have to be. Putting things bluntly, your father's your father and that's that. Uncle Mike recommends you give the man some credit. He may be more than a clueless antique sent by a universe that hates you for the sole purpose of ruining your life. There's a chance your father actually loves you and doesn't want you growing up on diet of misogyny (look it up), a Capella violence, and self-righteous nihilism masquerading as the art of social protest. Personally, Uncle Mike would gnaw off his own ears before listening to newly rich, recently paroled sociopaths snarling personal blank verse. Of course, he feels the same way about Kenny G. Everybody's a critic.

123

Dear Uncle Mike,

My girlfriend and I think you're really cool. We're sixteen and we want to know why okay guys hang out with slutty girls. I mean, is it just sex? Don't guys have to like the girl? Are guys really that dumb? Do they get smarter when they get older or are they just less obvious about it?

Two fans, Lincoln City

Dear Fans,

Uncle Mike would first like to say how much your letter brightened his day. Whenever people who've never met Uncle Mike, let alone wintered in a small cabin with him, write to say he's really cool, it always makes Uncle Mike smile, and then bury his face in his hands.

You ask why okay guys hang out with slutty girls. Let's define our terms. By 'okay guys', Uncle Mike guesses you mean adolescent males who are able to curb their unbridled lust at least part of the time, know how to use a fork, and are able to form complete sentences. By 'slutty girls', he assumes you mean adolescent females who use their sexuality to achieve personal and social goals, laugh too loudly, and pop their gum.

What draws these people together? There isn't a force in the universe strong enough to keep them apart. Unless we count self awareness and restraint, which we can't. Is it just sex that draws the males into the candle flame of merciless truth? Yes and no. Young males, and not a few older ones, tend to fall in love, at least briefly, with any female willing to have sex with them. Strange, but there it is. Is what they feel love? Maybe, maybe not. The toxic levels of testosterone sloshing through the systems of the most okay of young guys can blur the subtle distinctions between naked lust and a burning desire to pair bond.

Can guys really be that dumb? You bet. But then, it depends on what you mean by dumb. Uncle Mike is more than seven in dog years and has yet to witness, let alone experience, a meaningless relationship. Or, for that matter, a meaningless act. We're all just out here trying to figure out what it means to be human. One of life's less funny truths is that we learn more from our failure than our successes and some lessons are best learned while you're still young enough to bounce back. The first rule of the playground is that we all try to play nice. With luck, and our good wishes, the okay guys and slutty girls may teach each other something about love. Do guys get smarter as they get older? Some do, some don't. And the ones who do aren't always easier to train. When someone says there's no fool like an old fool, they're probably not talking about a woman.

●●●

Dear Uncle Mike,
       I read somewhere they've found out some of the stars are older than the universe. What does this mean?
                                        Confused in Eugene

Dear Confused,
       In nontechnical terms, it means someone figured wrong.

●●●

Letters to Uncle Mike

Dear Uncle Mike,

I'm writing about a buddy of mine. He's in his late thirties and his life's a mess. He hates his job, he drinks too much, he's depressed. Like the rest of us, he's had his share of troubles. But it's like he's forgotten how to have fun. The worst part is that he doesn't think he can change anything. The guy's got a lot going for him and I keep trying to cheer him up. Nothing seems to be working. Any advice?

James S., Portland

Dear Jim Bob,

Your friend's problem is spiritual. What you're describing is someone who's lost their faith. There's a lot of it going around. Uncle Mike's first suggestion would be for him to stop drinking. Strong drink, as someone pointed out, makes fools of men and robs them of their will. These are alcohol's great charms and, in all fairness, the results aren't always bad. Uncle Mike has had many moments of harmless epiphany celebrating nothing in particular with epic quantities of sour mash. But he eventually learned not to drink when the blackness was on him. He kept waking up with very bad poetry. Your friend is waking up with a bad novel.

Tell him for Uncle Mike that he's behaving like a nincompoop. On exactly what principle of the universe does he base his professed inability to change things? Deciding not to change things changes things. It has, for instance, made his life an unholy mess that's involving people who love him. Try pointing out the obvious. No matter how rotten his day's been, it's over. In all of creation, nothing's more dead than yesterday, and forcing yourself to live there, pouring over spilt milk, is not the act of a rational person. Remind your friend that the sun will rise tomorrow on a day no one's ever seen. Ask him where he gets off saying it's ugly before it's born.

Which brings us back to faith, without which the human comedy becomes a bad soap opera. How does your friend get it back? If nothing else, by pretending he never lost it. Act as if you have faith in something larger than your definition of yourself and faith, as one of the Carpenter from Galilee's scribes put it, will be granted to you. It doesn't matter who or what does the granting. Uncle Mike is no more Christian than he is Buddhist, and no more Buddhist than he is Quantum Cabalist, and none of them more than a Probabilistic Pantheist with strong Pythagorean leanings. He does know good advice when he hears it. Uncle Mike has seen no evidence refuting the notion that the world is the spirit made flesh. Or that, in terms of the world, we are what we do and our lives are the merciless reflection of it. If they're a mess, it's no accident. Since Uncle Mike has a hard time believing we're sinners in the hands of an angry God, when his life unravels he automatically suspects it's the result of something he's either done or not done. And darned if that's not always the case.

If your friend's been wallowing in self pity very long, and you should assure him that's just what it is, it may be time to play hardball. Remind him that he has a responsibility to himself and the people who love him to be the best human being he can. The nice thing about a spherical universe is that, no matter where you are, you can get where you want to go. We all do it one step at a time. When the going gets really tough, Uncle Mike starts wondering if the mess he's made of things isn't really beyond him this time, he falls back on one of life's noble truths: laughter is the purest form of revolution.

Letters to Uncle Mike

Dear Uncle Mike,

I respect your opinion and I was wondering what you think about the whole penis extension theory. As in, do men drive big, jacked up cars because their penises are little? What kind of a car do you drive?

Lucy in Eugene

Dear Lucy,

After much thought, Uncle Mike has backed away from the whole penis extension theory on the grounds that it fails to make distinctions between the penis as metaphor and the penis as actual appendage. Before going one inch further, Uncle Mike wants to make clear his stance on gender determined behavior. In terms of quantum physics, from which all manifestation flows, there are two modes of action in the universe: emission and absorption. They couldn't be more different. Their relationship is complementary, the pairing of unlikes. Much of the pain and sadness between male and female humans would go away if the principle of complementarity were taught in kindergarten.

Which brings us to testosterone and estrogen, the hormonal duality that reflects emission/absorption like a fun house mirror, and contributes so much to the human comedy. Uncle Mike's no rocket psychologist but, judging from what he's seen, over and over again and with his own eyes, testosterone predisposes males to emit (often inappropriately), and females to absorb (often too completely). The relationship implies no hierarchy, only difference, and the certainty of embarrassing abuses on both sides. Successful humans of either gender are marked by an ability to emit and absorb selectively, balancing the forces of nature in ways that make them pleasant dinner companions. It's dangerous to generalize, but it seems safe to say that male humans who drive big, jacked up cars are still laboring to achieve this balance.

Which brings us, nearly, to penises. Men, especially young ones, define themselves in terms of their extension in the world: the shadow they cast on the brick walls of whatever power system they've bought into. It's the penis as general principle, rather than the penis of fact, that revs its motor at stop lights, grins like an idiot on Prozac, and honks its horn. It (meaning the human the principle is operating through) does this because it hasn't a clue, is nervous as a stray cat, and feels any emission is better than none. The penis being extended is a mental construct, although in most cases this seems too much to expect of the men involved.

Now then, for the heart of your question. Is there a correlation between testosterone induced penile behavior and the actual anatomy of those who display it? Uncle Mike hasn't the foggiest notion. He's seen no published studies and, given the nature of the times, would be suspicious of any findings. We do know this: most young males, and some old enough to know better, worry unduly about their extension. (While you ladies are laughing and snorting, remember men have time to do this because they're not obsessing about their breasts.) Given this undercurrent of anxiety, one could say with reasonable confidence that men who drive oversized Tonka toys are making up for a real or imagined shortcoming. It's a funny world, one whose historians suggest that much of the past, especially its least pleasant episodes, can be explained in terms of males acting out issues of low self esteem. Uncle Mike has no quarrel with this theory.

You ask what sort of car Uncle Mike drives. He doesn't. Walking makes him feel almost adequate.

Letters to Uncle Mike

Dear Uncle Mike,

I'd feel stupid writing to Ann Landers, but I feel okay about writing to you. I'm 26, my girlfriend is 25. We've been living together for a year now. I really love her a lot and I know she loves me. The problem is she doesn't trust me. I work in the restaurant business and there are a lot of pretty women around. She knows I've got a lot of opportunities to mess around and is convinced I must be. I'm not. I've never really been tempted. I knew she was jealous before we moved in together but I thought it would get better the more she knew me. It's not. I think it's getting worse. She came in the other night and caught me talking to the bartender. Now she's convinced we've either done the big nasty or are thinking about it. You're an older guy. You've been around. What do you say to a suspicious woman to make her trust you?

Eddie in Eugene

Dear Eddie,

Uncle Mike would feel stupid writing to Ann Landers too, and is none too sure about the people who write to him. As a first step on your path to being trusted, Uncle Mike would suggest you change your name. Don't take this personally, but nowhere in western literature, including film and television, has there ever been a character named Eddie who could be trusted. Besides, you're 26 years old, and even if you wear your baseball cap backwards, you're a card carrying adult. Introduce yourself as Edward, or Ed. You should also vow never again to refer to making love, or even having sex, as 'doing the big nasty'.

What do you say to a suspicious woman to make her trust you? To begin with, the truth. You say your friend walked in and "caught" you talking to the bartender.

Interesting choice of words, Eddie. If you're telling the truth and have never "really even been tempted" (pardon Uncle Mike while he rolls his eyes), tell this truth often and in as many ways as possible. When's the last time you told the woman she was beautiful, that you couldn't imagine life without her, that you'd lie down in front of a stampeding herd of Mack trucks for her? When's the last time you meant it? You say there are a lot of pretty women in your workplace. This implies you've noticed. Uncle Mike trusts you don't 'notice' them when you're with the woman who should be the center of your attention. The casting of lascivious, or even appreciative, glances qualifies as suspicious behavior. Women are pretty silly, huh Eddie.

Now that we've drilled your teeth, let's start on hers. Life's a weird business and some folks have a hard time trusting any part of it. Women have a hard time trusting men because, when it comes to fidelity, men tend to be scoundrels and liars. You need to face the possibility that this woman is never going to trust you. Never. There must be harder things to work around in a relationship, but Uncle Mike (who is, as you pointed out, an older guy who's been around) hasn't an inkling what they'd be. The whole idea of love involves tearing down the owner-built walls that separate us, not just from our mates, but from the world. Trust is another word for faith; faith that the person you love would never intentionally hurt you. Unless you truly believe your partner would not, when push comes to shove, drive a stake through your heart, love's a real stretch. It's not, however, an impossible dream. It's no accident you're with this woman, Ed. Everyone's a teacher, everyone's a student. You teach her about trust, she teaches you about inspiring it. Cooperation, just like on Sesame Street.

Letters to Uncle Mike

Dear Uncle Mike,
Who was it who said "Blondes have more fun." Mae West or Jean Harlow?
Frannie S., Portland

Dear Frannie,
Uncle Mike has no idea. And, since he's not the information service at the library, he has no intention of rushing off into the stacks to find out. His guess would be it was either a brunette who was off her game or a blonde who had a hard time distinguishing between pleasure and excitement.

● ● ●

Dear Uncle Mike,
My boyfriend's being a pain. He says I should sip from the edge of the spoon instead of putting it in my mouth. He says it's just good table manners, I say it's stupid. What do you say?
Fed Up in Astoria

Dear Fed Up,
Off the top of his head, Uncle Mike would say your friend's an effete twit who should be encouraged to eat alone. Of all the things thoughtful humans have to think about in the last minutes of the twentieth century, your pretentious patrician wannabe is troubled by the way someone else uses a spoon. One wonders whether to laugh or to cry. In a kinder, gentler world, someone would snatch him from the table and drop him naked on the sidewalks of Calcutta.

132

Table manners are one thing, Byzantine food rituals are another. Having suffered through his share of overly decorous dining, Uncle Mike (who doesn't belch and knows which fork to use with his stir fry) is convinced the art of complicated eating was invented by people with too much time on their hands, inflated feelings of self worth, and a naked urge to make others feel like slobs. Uncle Mike would bet they were French.

As for you and your spoon, granted the usual rules of decorum, you have Uncle Mike's permission to do with it what you will. He resists the temptation to suggest a rude action involving your friend.

● ● ●

Dear Uncle Mike,

I got woke up again the other night by somebody's car alarm. Isn't this disturbing the peace?
                                        A Victim in Cannon Beach

Dear Victim,

Absolutely. Unless you count the law. Paraphrasing the police person Uncle Mike talked to recently around midnight, speaking loudly enough to drown out the claxon horn of someone's personal auto security system: "If it were your car, you'd feel differently about the noise." No, Uncle Mike wouldn't. Even if Uncle Mike owned a car, he'd expect the metal brute to fend for itself and not be a nuisance when left alone. If it woke the neighbors, Uncle Mike would scold it and then rip out the offending circuitry.

But this is America and, thanks to the lobbying efforts of those who manufacture car alarm systems, any moron can have one. Never mind that the decibel level exceeds most community's noise abatement statutes; never mind that car theft is one of the reasons God made insurance companies; never mind that, judging from the sound of things, the owners scarcely leap up from their bar stools or beds to check if the machine doing the shrieking is theirs. There should at least be a law making car alarms personalized. Uncle Mike would feel a little better hearing: "Dan and Julie! Wake up!

It's your car! Someone's trying to...aargh!" No, that's a lie. He'd still want to reach for his scatter gun.

Which brings us to America's current passion: leveling the playing field or, as it used to be called, getting even. If someone's personal siren three blocks away wakes Uncle Mike up, Uncle Mike should be allowed to put on his pants, walk up quietly and beat it senseless with a ball bat. Or, as an alternative, the law should supply Uncle Mike with the owner's home address so that, some night when he's feeling insecure, he could set up a public address system on their front lawn and do dramatic readings from the works of James Joyce. Uncle Mike has never denied his mean streak.

● ● ●

Dear Uncle Mike,

Quite a spell ago, I made an innocent inquiry of a Seaside cafe employee (former mayor of same). From that moment I perceived a decided stiff and cold shoulder. I simply asked for the distance to Cannon, and could I expect to have a non-excessive walk to there. My question to you, Uncle Mike, is this: have there been 'words' between Seaside and Cannon Beach?

David L., Portland

Dear Dave,

Not so many lately. The little they had to say to each other has long since been said. The relationship between Seaside and Cannon Beach has found its own level, a level Uncle Mike would characterize as mutual loathing, and communication between them now is almost entirely by rumor. All for the best since, aside from being populated by air breathers, few municipalities have less in common. Cannon Beach enjoys (or, if you're from Seaside, wallows in) an artistic tradition dating back several decades, a tradition currently preserved by a vacationing class willing to pay $200 a night for a motel room and buy objects d'art at prices exceeding that of a good used car. Seaside has bumper cars, corn dogs, and street crime and thinks anybody who doesn't is an artsy-fartsy wuss. Reconciliation isn't likely. Cannon Beach is much too busy being at one with itself to discuss things with people who drink coffee without Mexican chocolate sprinkles and wear t-shirts that say rude things. Seaside would sooner drive its Camaro into a tree than party with those who read the New Yorker, sniff wine corks, and use big words. It was a kind universe that placed the towns nine miles apart. A kinder one wouldn't have built a road between them.

● ● ●

135

Letters to Uncle Mike

Dear Uncle Mike,

I have a woman friend I've known for several years. We've been close since we met but lately we're getting closer. We're both in our mid forties, I'm single, her marriage is sucking big time. Over the years, we've talked about other people crossing the line and how our friendship meant so much to us because we didn't. Now it looks like it might, or at least could. I've always thought her husband was a jerk, so there's no loyalty issue there. She just needs someone and I care about her, maybe more than I realized, or in a deeper way. I don't expect you to solve my dilemma but I would be interested in your thoughts.

Leaning in Astoria

Dear Leaning,

Basically, Uncle Mike just has one. The woman is married. That her marriage is troubled and her husband a jerk are details, not extenuating circumstances. It also doesn't matter that, given your feelings for each other, you'd be making love instead of rooting around like a pair of weasels in heat. It doesn't even matter that the comfort and compassion you could give might deepen both your friendship and her marriage, although this plot development is more common in cheap novels than real life. All that matters is that this woman made a vow and your only option as a friend is to do everything in your power to help her keep it. If her marriage is over, she needs to get out of it. If not, she needs to get on with it. What the two of you need to do is reaffirm your vows of personal integrity. In the meantime, light a candle. Every time you have lascivious thoughts about your friend, hold your hand over the flame until you can't stand it. It's an old technique guaranteed to steady the will.

Dear Uncle Mike,

I just started reading your column and I think I'm in love. Are you married? Do you have a girlfriend or something? Are you heterosexual? Would you like to have dinner and drinks?

Amy J., Portland

Dear Amy,

Uncle Mike is glad you read his column and even more glad that you're in love. Uncle Mike is a great fan of love. Along with playing poker, it's the glue that holds him together. Is Uncle Mike married? Only to the few principles he has left. Is Uncle Mike heterosexual? Devoutly. Unless you count the night when, after several hundred gin and tonics, he grew suddenly fond of a female impersonator. Does Uncle Mike have a girlfriend or something? Uncle Mike is too old to have a girlfriend. It makes his friends worry. Uncle Mike does have 'something' but, being shy, he declines to say what it is. Would Uncle Mike like to have dinner and drinks? Sadly, since we've never met, neither of us could hope to know. Perhaps, if you dropped by on visiting day, we could sit in the game room and talk.

● ● ●

Dear Uncle Mike,

You wrote something once about death and physics, how there couldn't be any really because the universe is always conscious. I think that's what you said. I was going to save it, but I didn't. Anyway, what about love

137

and physics? A friend told me she heard that Einstein said that gravity wasn't love. If it isn't, what is? I'm 18 and would really like to know.

Emily in Portland

Dear Emily,

Uncle Mike thinks Einstein was right and can only imagine how excited he'd be to hear it. Newton's gravitation was the mysterious attraction every piece of the universe has for every other. Relativistic gravitation is the curvature of space/time, the impersonal urge the universe has to curl up and be one with its navel. Neat as they both are, neither one are love. Uncle Mike sees love as phase entanglement.

To review the basics. The universe is a four dimensional ripple tank. Observed reality is a standing wave pattern on a sea of unevoked possibility and we are wave packets: the sum and product of the invisible waves of our atoms stirred by invisible electrons dancing around our nuclei in the moonlight. Each human wave form is unique, a grand chord played on the ripple pond of awareness. The billions upon billions of waves making up the chord began when the universe first blinked and have been waving steadily ever since.

Here comes the good part. Every time a wave interacts with another wave, both are forever altered, each of them going away with a different energy and orientation, a little piece of the other's heart. The universe is a garden of interpenetrating wave forms, giggling and singing and skipping along, leaving bits of themselves with everyone they meet, taking bits to remember each other by. That's phase entanglement, a quantum intimacy exactly as old as time.

So much for mathematical elves and faeries. In the

larger picture you have us: finely tuned wave packets organized around a point conscious perspective which, like the waves that ripple reality, has existed.

Leaving the world of mathematical elves and faeries for the world of observed events, you have us: finely tuned wave packets who recognize potential harmony with other wave packets.

In the larger picture, you have us: human wave packets humming and whistling around a point conscious perspective, the much talked about 'I'. At our best we're extremely fine-tuned and recognize right off the potential for harmony with other wave packets. That's love, Uncle Mike experiences it a lot when he drinks sour mash, and it exists to a greater or lesser degree, as an intrinsic relationship between all things. Some waves augment us, others interfere. The more the harmony, the more intricate the phase relationships and the deeper the resonance. Just like love, harmony depends upon difference. Harmony is the unification of difference balancing differences.

● ● ●

Dear Uncle Mike,

My girlfriend and I broke up a few months ago. We were together, not living together but dating exclusively, for a little over a year. The breakup was mutual. We both thought it was time to do other things, see other people. We're both 29 by the way. We talk on the phone a lot and try to get together for dinner or drinks once a week. To make a long story short, I'm falling in love with her again.

She's seeing someone else but the impression I get is that it's not the love of her life or anything even though they sleep together. I asked her one night if she ever thought about getting back together. She got this really nice smile on her face and said no, not for a while anyway. But her eyes and smile said different. I'm not seeing anyone now and I'm starting to not want to start a new relationship in case she makes up her mind. It's been a month now. If you were in my shoes, what would you do?

Brian

Dear Brian,

Uncle Mike would tap himself on the forehead with a mallet.

Brian, Brian, Brian. Sit down and look at things as they are. You and this woman dated for a year without moving in together. Since the breakup was mutual, we must assume a measurable distance has always been part of your relationship. Personal space, free to be me sort of thing. From this less than epic romance you moved on to greater personal space, other things, and other people. Let Uncle Mike know when he's going astray.

So, being modern and with it, you maintain your friendship. For several months, during which time she finds a new lover and you don't. You're feeling lonely and left out, she's not. Things clearing up yet, Brian Bob? So, in a grand display of humiliation, you ask if she's interested in rekindling the matchstick of your former love. Like Uncle Mike, you should have a hard time believing you did this. But you did. And what did the woman say? She said no. Can you say 'over', Brian?

You get the impression her new man isn't the love of her life. If she actually said this, you failed to mention it in your letter. Maybe she doesn't choose to share breathless descriptions of her love life with you. Good for her. If Uncle Mike were sitting across the table from an old love who was making cow eyes over the pasta, he'd find other things to talk about too.

But she said no with her lips and yes with her eyes, right? That's odd behavior all by itself, babe. And it's been a month now and she hasn't said an encouraging word. And you're moping around in your bathrobe waiting for this woman to make up her mind? While Uncle Mike admires your ability to endure without hope, he thinks you're acting like a character in a painful Woody Allen film. He suggests you stop it.

● ● ●

Dear Uncle Mike,

Relative to car alarms: I would consider supporting a rule that car alarms had to have a time limit and if the owner didn't turn it off, the doors would automatically unlock and the car would start. The only thing I see against this rule is I think there are too many rules and so I have trouble promoting a new one. But, if we could trade this in for some other rule, a bad rule, then I could support it. Hey! That should be a rule: Any new rule must include removing some existing rule. This would help to promote: "Not More Rules, Better Rules". I like it. It reads like a bumper sticker.

Sincerely,
Victoria F.

Dear V,

Your idea is a dandy. Uncle Mike senses in you a kindred spirit and warns you not to forget to take your medicine. Any rule that undermines the notion of personal responsibility is, on Uncle Mike's block, a bad rule. Car alarms should only be activated when the owner snaps on a collar sheathed with a highly conductive metal. The moment someone tampers with his or her personal driving machine, a stiff but nonlethal jolt of electricity awakens them and persists, relentlessly, until they go turn it off. As long as Uncle Mike knows they're in pain, he can live with the sirens.

• • •

Dear Uncle Mike,

Here's a question for you. How do you stop falling in love with the wrong woman? Over and over again. I always start out thinking this is the one I've been waiting for. I always end up dealing with somebody I only thought I knew who has habits that drive me crazy or gross me out. Is there part of this I'm not getting? I know the kind of woman I want. Why can't they be what they seem? Maybe it's me. But if love is blind, how do people stay together?

Confused in Eugene

Dear Confused,

You neglected to tell Uncle Mike how old you are. Judging from the thrust of your questions, he'd guess you're about twelve and will answer as simply as he can.

How does one stop falling in love with the wrong

women? One way is to know who you are, as opposed to who you imagine yourself to be. You can expect this to take most of your life. Another thing you want to do is learn the difference between what you want and what you need. What you want is what you don't have. What you need is what's yours.

Karma being what it is, falling in love with the wrong person is a term without meaningful referents. Uncle Mike would encourage you to look up 'cause and effect' in your Funk and Wagnall's and see how much room it leaves for 'mistakes'. The women in your life come to deliver a teaching and learning you're behaving like a stupid wart is seldom fun. Uncle Mike always counsels himself to eat the pain and leave a large tip. Avoid falling in love with women you don't like. Hormonal lunacy is fun and all, but unless you're in love with pain and sadness, you should look for the same qualities in your lovers that you look for in your friends. Hopefully, this won't include drinking beer from the pitcher and behaving like swine.

The transformation phenomena you speak of, in which someone who holds your heart in their hand changes from a source of pleasure and fulfillment to one of surprise and shocked disbelief, is nature's way of reminding us to laugh. Listen carefully, cupcake. No one is what you think they are. They are, simultaneously, much more and much less than you or they imagine. That's why we call them humans. Is love blind? Uncle Mike doesn't think so. Uncle Mike thinks love has the eyes of a hawk and all the mercy of a puff adder. How do people stay together? With varying degrees of difficulty and generous helpings of faith. Like everything else in the universe, love is an act of creation, something we make up as we go along. To paraphrase our great teacher, Dylan of Minnesota, love not busy being born is busy dying. You'll understand if and when you grow up.

Dear Uncle Mike,

My ten year old son wants a pet tarantula. I like to encourage his interests but to be honest with you, the things give me the creeps. Do spiders make good pets? How much space do they need? What do you feed them? Can they be de-fanged? The guy at the pet store says tarantulas are really interesting and no trouble at all. Have you ever been around one? Am I being phobic?

Chris L., Portland

Dear Chris,

A commonly overlooked fact about phobias is that they're firmly grounded in good sense. Fear of heights comes from a knowledge of gravity and the truth that there's nothing between you and the ground but thin air. Fear of pit bulls comes from an unwillingness to be torn apart and eaten by something with more teeth than brains. Fear and loathing of spiders is the racial memory of having one jump onto your face.

Do spiders make good pets? Not unless you enjoy living with a nightmare. It takes a special sort of person to watch Seinfeld with a tarantula curled up on his lap. With luck, your son isn't this far gone. Do they need much space? Like anything else, spiders will take as much space as they can get. If you're smart, this will be no larger than a small aquarium with a large rock on the lid. As far as diet is concerned, your spider will eat anything it can pick apart with its ghoulish mandibles. Given sufficient appetite, you and your son will fall into this category. Can tarantulas be de-fanged? Absolutely. The proper tool is a large mallet.

●●●

Dear Uncle Mike,

My boyfriend and I are have a question we need settled. Who was it who said, "Let them eat cake"? He says it was Madame Pompadour, I say Marie Antoinette. Do you know?

Rebecca in Astoria

Dear Rebecca,

It's usually attributed to Marie Antoinette, but she didn't say it either. Nothing even close, in fact. Uncle Mike suspects it was Sara Lee.

●●●

Dear Uncle Mike,

Einstein said gravity isn't love. If it's not, what is?

Curious in Seattle

Dear Curious,

First off, Uncle Mike would like to thank you for writing. Knowing there's at least one human in Seattle who thinks about something more than what flavor of latte to have for the high velocity commute to the virtual factory where legions of young millionaires devise new ways to patent freedom of information cheers Uncle Mike greatly. You must be lonely.

When it comes to love in a quantum universe, Uncle Mike agrees with Einstein, a stance that's paid off in the past. According to general relativity, gravity is a topographical map of a space/time warped by mass. Pretty as this is, it's not, even to the desperate, the stuff of romance. The love/gravity connection comes from the equations of classical physics, in which Newton (Isaac, not Olivia) described gravitation as the universal attraction every bit of mass in the universe has for every other. In either view, the moon loves the earth, the earth loves the sun, and everything loves black holes. Gravity is more like lust: discreet masses behaving indiscriminately. If gravity were love, we'd all live in the mountains and have daydreams about lead.

(Note: Just because relativistic gravitation reflects the universe's urge to curl up with itself and achieve dimensionless unity, it's not the source of mystical love either. That feeling of oneness is phase entanglement, the flip side of gravity in which every photon's waveform is the product of every other waveform it's encountered since the beginning of space/time.)

Okay, so what's love? Uncle Mike thinks its resonance. Resonance (from the Latin: to sound again) is the vibration induced in a body by the vibration of another body. Uncle Mike's body, and yours, is an electromagnetic event. The little iron atoms in the blood circulate, the little synapses fire, we wonder about love. DNA being the impressive alphabet it is, no two human circuits are alike. In Seattle terms, the hardware's fairly consistent, but the software's random. Our operating frequency is a reflection of who we are and how we relate to and interact with the world. Some people, for instance, like Barry Manilow and believe Bill Gates likes them.

So there we are, vibrating at a rate determined by an organizing principle which, for want of a better term, we'll call our spirit. All vibrations effect us, we either like professional wrestling or we don't. Resonance occurs when the frequency of the oscillation matches our own and our strings begin to vibrate. In extreme cases, or after several gin rickeys, there's an unsettling free fall in the abdomen as the iron atoms dance little polar shifts.

Love that lasts longer than the warranty on an average new car reflects an intricate mix of commonalties and contrasts that, instead of damping our circuits, augments them. Love is the only sum greater than its parts. When we love and are loved, we become more of who we are. Love is the art, and the wisdom, of taking all that's offered and giving all you have. It's nice it's no more complicated than humming along with the music and listening for harmony.

● ● ●

Dear Uncle Mike,

My boyfriend and I have been living together for about a year. I thought everything was fine. Then two months ago an old girlfriend of mine moved back to town. We've been seeing a lot of her. Maybe too much. She's really good looking and has always been a flirt. Lately I don't like the way the two of them are together. When she comes over for dinner, the good-bye hugs are lasting a little too long. Brad says I'm imagining things. She laughs and says I'm being silly. I'm not sure what to do. What would you do?

Worried in Astoria

Dear Worried,

The first thing Uncle Mike would do is stop worrying. What you're looking for is the truth. Invite the little trollop over for dinner and observe how much your dog of a boyfriend wags his tail. When the meals over and the coffee's poured, put on your coat. Tell them you're off to spend the night in a hotel so they'll have a chance to discuss issues of hormones and loyalty and won't be disturbed by the sight of you putting your fingers down your throat.

● ● ●

Dear Uncle Mike,
You've talked about death before, how it doesn't exist according to quantum physics, whatever the hell that is. Would you mind running it by me again? Someone in my circle died recently and I could use some perspective.
Grieving in Cannon Beach

Dear Friend,
Uncle Mike is always happy to talk about death. It's one of those subjects that, the more you think about it, the better you feel. Uncle Mike doesn't believe in death for two reasons. First, because he sees no evidence of it in the physical world. Second, because, in its popular form, there's no room for it in the equations.
Keeping matters simple, the 'I' we see in the mirror is a complex waveform. Like a chord strummed on the electric guitar of the universe, our bodies are the surface features of an energy field. We are, in this way, brothers and sisters of everything, from seashells to scotch terriers, tennis shoes to philodendra, sunsets to stars. The observable we is what Buckminster Fuller called a 'pattern integrity', a slip knot that slides through space-

148

time, a one of a kind ripple on the pond of current events.

Owing to biochemical processes too disgusting to talk about, our body ripples eventually fade and disappear. This is, of course, an illusion. The conservation laws governing mass/energy and momentum are very firm about life everlasting in a closed four-dimensional ripple tank. Things change; they don't 'go away'. There's nowhere for them to go. Uncle Mike can hear you saying that, in terms of being able to have lunch with friends, dead is still dead. Uncle Mike would agree if it weren't for the notion of pattern integrities.

Your spirit is a pattern integrity, an organizing principle dropped, constantly and forever, into the formless potential of life. Slip knots sliding through space/time. Minor chords in the unfinished symphony of the universe. Put another way, imagine a glass sphere. Every point inside the sphere is a perspective. The sum of all the point perspectives, an infinite number of them, is the internal reality of the sphere. If any of the perspectives disappeared, the geometry of the sphere would collapse. In terms of the geometry of space/time, you and Uncle Mike are point conscious perspectives that generate biological fields that shave, belch, and have social security numbers. We were born to do this. And, because all perspectives existed, as potential, in the first nanosecond of the big bang, our perspectives have a) always been here, and b) always will be. Subtract even one and the universe ceases to exist. This is probably what they call the sting of death.

● ● ●

Letters to Uncle Mike

Dear Uncle Mike,

Enclosed is an article I received in the mail from (name withheld to prevent nondivine retribution). This born-again Christian lives about six blocks from me, but I have never met him. He sends me letters from time to time trying to convert me to Christianity, but I'm a heathen that does not believe the Bible is the word of God.

The article headed "World Events and Bible Prophecy" says that scientists have discovered the actual location of Hell which is nine miles below the earth. I think it is hogwash, but I would like to have your expert opinion. I fully understand if you do not wish to reply to such a stupid article, but with you sense of humor and knowledge you just might want to.

I read your reply to a person that wanted to know about death, and I think it was magnificent. I look forward to your monthly column and the Upper Left Edge.

Best regards from an old freethinker.

J.C. Sammons, Portland

Dear J.C.,

Uncle Mike is pleased that you look forward to his column and the Upper Left Edge, the only non-newspaper in the nation with the taste and lack of forethought to publish it. As soon as Uncle Mike finishes answering your letter, he plans to rummage through the back issues looking for signs of magnificence. He's pretty darned excited.

As for the discovery of hell, Uncle Mike must, even in the face of the startling new evidence you've sent along, suspend his judgment. This isn't to say he doesn't value scientific bulletins from The End Times and Victorious Living. He does, if only for the incredible leaps of faith they encourage. In the their own way, they're inspiring.

According to the report, a group of reported scientists were, for reasons not reported, drilling a nine mile deep hole in "remote Siberia". At an undisclosed depth, the drill bit "started to spin madly." The scientists took this as proof that the Earth is hollow. The report says they were "dumbfounded". Uncle Mike fears it may have been worse than that. It certainly got no better when they measured the temperature and found it to be 2,000 degrees Fahrenheit (1,100 Celsius), much more than they expected. Echoing the understanding of many high school graduates: "It seems almost like an inferno of fire is brutally going on in the center of the earth." 'Brutal' is a scientific term too sticky to get into.

So there they are, in "remote Siberia", with a wildly spinning drill bit and a fiery inferno from the pages of a geology textbook. Saints preserve us. Pushing their luck, the scientists lowered a microphone into the hole to listen for earth movements, a phenomenon of which they were miraculously aware. "What we heard turned those logically thinking scientists into a trembling ruins." No, not a paradigm shift. "We heard a human voice, screaming in pain. Even though one voice was discernible, we could hear thousands, perhaps millions, in the background, of suffering souls screaming." To their credit, it's reported that: "We could hardly believe our own ears." Sadly, they seem to have managed. "After the terrible discovery, half of the scientists have quit because of their fear." Of enduring another day in remote Siberia?

No. Having heard "screams of condemned souls" coming from "the world's deepest hole", the scientists "are afraid that they have released the evil powers of hell to the surface of the earth." As well they should.

Aside from being a heady spiritual responsibility, it

would also be a subject of intense interest to someone's insurance company. On the bright side, it would be grounds for winning the first, and last, Nobel Prize for metaphysics.

Like you, Uncle Mike considers himself a freethinker and, in a strictly Pythagorean sense, a heathen. All things are possible, some of them are just infinitely less possible than others. If, as The End Times and Victorious Living deduces from the evidence, "Hell is No Joke!"; and if Uncle Mike is perched on the slippery edge of a fiery pit opened by some hapless nitwits in remote Siberia, so be it. There is a silver lining. As Uncle Mike's learned editor, Reverend Billy Bob points out: If the Earth is round, we're always nine miles from hell. If you live in Cannon Beach, Seaside is two miles closer. And there are bumper cars.

● ● ●

Dear Uncle Mike,

I get jealous about my boyfriend being around other women. Is jealousy a sin?

Jealous in Lincoln City

Dear Jealous,

Technically speaking, no. Certainly not if he's doing something to warrant your suspicion. The sort of jealousy you're talking about is a mental imbalance suffered by those who believe in the notion of emotional property rights.

Dear Uncle Mike,

I read your column all the time and you sound pretty cool so I thought I'd write and ask your advice. I'm 17 and will graduate this year. My grades are good and I don't get into trouble. The only problem I have is my boyfriend. Or rather my parents. He's 22 and my folks think he's too old for me. He's not. We love each other and do lots of stuff together.

It's not like I'm going to run off and get married. Does our age difference really matter? What do you think? I promise I'll listen.

Kirsten in Lake Oswego

Dear Kirsten,

Uncle Mike is glad you think he's pretty cool. There are those who would tell you, you're young and have much to learn.

Does age difference really matter? All things being relative, it depends. As any used car salesman will tell you, it's not the age, it's the mileage. There are 17 year olds Uncle Mike would trust with his car, if he had one. There are 22 year olds who need instructions to chew gum. The issue is maturity, a boring word that means having the experience necessary to make sound decisions. One of the soundest decisions you can make is to listen to your elders. Especially those who know and love you.

Uncle Mike is glad to hear of your lack of plans to marry. It reminds him of one of the many parables of poker. There are good hands, there are bad hands, and it's a long game.

● ● ●

153

Letters to Uncle Mike

Dear Uncle Mike,

Do you think they're going to legalize marijuana? I know you're in favor of it. Why? Have you tested its effects on yourself?

Brad in Portland

Dear Nosey,

Does Uncle Mike think 'they' are going to legalize marijuana? No, that would involve a loss of face. They're just going to make it available to anyone who can demonstrate signs of stress. Yes, Uncle Mike is in favor of this. As a human, Uncle Mike thinks he should be able to eat, drink, snort, or smoke anything that grows in the garden. He also believes he is the sole caretaker of his body. Has Uncle Mike tested the effects of marijuana on himself? Yes, many times. It's what makes him drive cars into trees and rob 7-Elevens.

● ● ●

Dear Uncle Mike,

Why do people sniff wine corks?

Unenlightened in Astoria

Dear Unenlightened,

Because Uncle Mike knows no one who does, he's unable to say. He does know people who look to see if the cork is damp. Uncle Mike can't remember if it's supposed to be or not. Even now, he doesn't care. He drinks sour mash whiskey and so, doesn't have to.

Dear Uncle Mike,

Is there proper bathroom etiquette when people spend the night? When you're ready for bed, should you offer your guests first use, or leave the bathroom for them after you've retired? I know it's not an earthshaking issue but I was just curious.

Mariah M., Portland

Dear Mariah,

Uncle Mike whimpers at the thought of anyone imagining an issue exists. People he knows well enough to let them sleep in his home go to the bathroom when they need to and go to bed when they're tired. If your guests start yawning (something Uncle Mike would bet happens a lot) and you're sitting on their hide-a-bed, by all means go brush your teeth and give it a rest.

● ● ●

Dear Uncle Mike,

A long time ago, you mentioned three rules for living on the planet. I forgot what they were. Sorry.

Melissa A.

Dear Melissa,

It's okay, not to worry, don't let it happen again. The rules you refer to are Reverend Billy's. Three Rules for Peace in the Universe: 1) nobody hits, 2) everybody eats, 3) there is no third rule.

To this, Uncle Mike would add a corollary: we get to love whoever we want.

155

There are also, just in case, Reverend Billy's 'Three Rules for Surviving on the Planet': Never play poker with anyone named Doc, never eat at a place called 'Mom's', and never sleep with anyone crazier than you are.

About the Author

Michael Burgess is an author and columnist of indeterminate age who observes the human comedy from the safety of a small town on the Oregon Coast. A prize winning journalist, he was, for ten years, featured columnist for *This Week Magazine* in Portland and served as founding president of *Northwest Writers, Inc.*, the region's first organization for those who, ignoring the pleas of family and friends, insist on arranging words for a living. He currently writes two syndicated columns: Ask Uncle Mike, a weekly advice column for the especially desperate, and Blame It On The Stars, a monthly horoscope for those who never read them. He is the author of four books: *'Magic and Magicians', 'Uncle Mike's Guide to the Real Oregon Coast'. Letters to Uncle Mike', and 'MORE Letters to Uncle Mike'.* He likes many dogs and some children, prefers briefs to boxers and, in his largely unbroken blocks of spare time, continues his search for a unified field equation suitable for printing on a T-shirt.

Also by the Author:

Uncle Mike's Guide to the Real Oregon Coast
ISBN: 0-9657638-1-1 ($14.95)

There are many pretty guides to the Oregon Coast. This isn't one of them. The author is a native Oregonian who assumes you want the truth. An overly zealous travel industry, and the shameless lies of tourists too proud to admit their mistakes, have created a myth of the Oregon Coast as a holiday destination for the normal to silly, if not dangerous, proportions.

The author refuses to be part of this. He has no axes to grind, no rain gear or sedatives to sell. He doesn't care if you visit the Oregon Coast or not. He only wants the pain and sadness to end. His heart goes out to the gullible who flock here each year expecting things they'll never find: warmth, sunlight, some token shred of civilization. He sees them as victims of a cruel joke. It's one thing to live in a fool's paradise, another to travel great distances getting to it.

More Letters to Uncle Mike
ISBN: 0-9657638-6-2 ($14.00)

More wisdom and ridicule from Uncle Mike, the Oregon Coast's sobering answer to Ann Landers and Dear Abby. Less mannerly than Miss Manners, more blunt than Dr. Ruth, Uncle Mike is the victim society's worst nightmare: someone who believes we're the product of the decisions we make, however laughable and wrongheaded. As Uncle Mike loves to remind us, it's not called the human comedy for nothing. If you still have questions about life, love, the seven deadly mistakes, the necessity of relationships, the therapeutic power of poker, or the role of the point conscious observer in a universe that makes itself up as it goes along, you've come to the right place.

Magic and Magicians
(Out of Print)

Published by Capstone Press

An introduction to magic and illusion for young readers

Uncle Mike's books are available at your local bookstore,
or order from:

Saddle Mountain Press
PO Box 1096
Cannon Beach, Oregon 97110
Phone (503) 436-2947
Fax (503) 436-8635

Email saddlemountain@upperleftedge.com